WHAT WILL BECOME OF US?

Counting Down To y2k

Edited by Julian Gregori

What Will Become of Us?

Counting Down To y2k

Printed in the United States of America

Published in association with the Literary Agency of
The Academic Freedom Foundation
108 Deerwood Road
Gerrardstown, WV 25420

Observations and quotations by professionals featured in this book
are their own opinions and do not necessarily reflect the views
of those professionals' employers.
None of the opinions in this resource book,
including those of the editor, are published as
financial, investment, legal or medical advice,
but strictly as journalistic opinion.

**Neither the Editor nor Publisher have business or financial
connections to any of the products or services
recommended in this book.**

Additional copies of this book may be ordered by credit card at this
orders-only number: 1- 800-771-2147, extension **85.**

ISBN 1-892709-00-7

CONTENTS

NOTICE

*Readers who can invest the time
to read only a small part of this book
would be advised to read
Chapters 8 and 9.*

*Important
additions and updates
to this book will be posted
on the internet at*

www.ethell.com/y2k/y2k.html

Acknowledgements

"... I write to alert you to a problem which could have extreme negative ...consequences. The 'Year 2000 Virus. '... I first learned of all this in February (1996) and requested a study by the Congressional Research Service. **The study...substantiates the worst fears of the doomsayers.** *The computer has been a blessing; if we don't act quickly, however, it could become the curse of the age."*

Letter from Senator Moynihan to
President Clinton, from the
Congressional Record, August 11, 1996

The first experts to issue warnings about y2k received no small amount of scorn. They were railed against as alarmists and doomsayers, but they responded by quietly presenting hard evidence for their predictions, many of which were proven correct as early as 1996. Yet the press continues to be slow, blind and incompetent. Writer Robert Samuelson, an exception, explained why in a May, 1998 *Washington Post* article.

"For the press," he writes, "I grasp the difficulties of covering this story. It's mostly hypothetical. Until we have a corpse, we don't know whether there's been a murder. Anyone writing about [y2k] now is shoved uneasily toward one of two polar positions: reassuring complacency (fixes will be made) or hysterical alarmism (the world will collapse).

"...I lean toward alarmism because all the specialists I contacted last week -- people actually involved with fixing computers -- are alarmed. On the record, they say the problem is serious and the hour is late. Their cheeriest view is that "no one knows" what will happen. Off the record they incline toward Doomsday."

In the same story Samuelson pleads guilty to journalistic incompetence for ignoring this story for so long.

We wish to thank the other journalists who, like Samuelson, began admitting the severity of the problem when they realized what the evidence shows. We thank the computer experts who told the truth about it. We especially want to acknowledge the early and courageous efforts of computer programmers and authors Ed Yourdon and Peter deJager, and economist and historian Dr. Gary North, who was the first to illustrate the connections between potential social, political and economic disorders and specific computer meltdowns.

We want to thank the dozens of programmers who explained their findings to us directly, with a special emphasis of appreciation for Dr. Michael Harden of Century Technologies and Dr. "Z", who wishes to remain nameless because he is working now as a special emergency advisor to the U.S. Congress.

Today there is still scorn for those who express concerns for a problem no one wants to think about. The most common objection is that "Only a very small handful of people have any concern. Therefore the danger can't be real."

The fact is there are thousands of computer professionals who share the same concerns. What is especially interesting about those who research y2k *thoroughly* is that they almost always arrive at the same conclusions and see the same dangers. It is those who do not do their homework and who do not contemplate the evidence who maintain a naive optimism that "the danger can't be real," or "those guys sounding the alarm are only doing it because they're making money off of FUD." FUD is the new depending on me to provide for them and to protect them from bad things, and the y2k bug may be the most dangerous thing to come along in a long time.

The challenges I faced when I started my business are nothing compared to the challenges I'll face if I have to survive a complex, 21st Century emergency. The y2k problem was not in my business plan or in my plans for my family, and I certainly never wanted to think about any of the scary stuff in this book. Prior to this pending problem I had never stockpiled any food, had never owned a gun, and had never had to change careers.

I'm not a pessimist. I'm one of those guys who never put a first aid kit in his car (even though I know I should have). I always shrugged off potential danger and believed disasters happen to other people or in movies. But y2k is not that kind of disaster. It's something unique. Even people like me have got to pay attention to this one. I think Americans can handle this problem pretty well if we're given all the facts, if we have a few days to let the consequences sink in, and then if we act on our conclusions. Americans are creative and resourceful, and the more facts we have the better we can come up with a plan of attack to deal with this setback.

This book outlines some of the more important facts. Here's the bottom line fact: *As creative and resourceful as the American people are, we can't wait for a miracle cure for this computer problem.*

The most ingenious software tool our programmers can imagine would fix only about 15 percent of the problem. The rest has to be done by hard, boring, grunt-work. The work is taking longer than even the experts predicted, and that's why one hears them talk about "when" the big computers fail, not "if" the big computers fail. The computer programmers are dealing the best they can with the problem, and someday they will have the problem totally fixed. But the fix won't come in time. The computers that fail will disrupt life in the US as we know it. Some people will be hurt. You will be one of those who are hurt unless you get ready. So get ready.

Ready for what? Ready for the hardships outlined by this book. Some careers will come to an end. Y2k has already set many businesses back millions of dollars in money they've been forced to spend in the hope that the expense will allow them to stay in business for a few more years. The financial effects of this problem alone will change the economy and hurt some of us pretty badly.

Even worse is the technological impact of the problem. This y2k computer "virus" holds lots of surprises. Even if some computers seem to be totally fixed, other computers might mess up the work of the very best programmers in the world. The "fixed" computers could possibly become "unfixed" in the blink of an eye. If those computers run important things like bank transactions or electrical power distribution, lots of people will be hurt all at once.

Some communities will have a terrible time getting by. But if enough people are prepared we can handle most difficulties with integrity, courage, resourcefulness, and charity toward those who are hurt worse than we are. I happen to have a number of friends who think the y2k problem might be one of the most fortuitous things that could happen to America, but only if its distresses don't catch us off guard.

Some of us might be forced to take the lengthy vacations we need, or to refocus our attention on our families we have been neglecting. Some of us will learn new trades and completely shift our career plans. We will rethink our priorities. Many of us will begin to live the lifestyles we need, rather than those we thought we wanted. When the schools and malls close, our young people may discover real life for the first time in their lives. The crisis might affect our diet in healthy ways, too. Fast food stores might go out of business. Fruit and grain might be all we can get to eat for a while.

Most importantly of all, many of us may learn what it means to free and independent; not "beholden" to certain technologies whose success or failure is beyond our control. How long has it been since American families have enjoyed that freedom?

My daughters, who like to read and re-read the Laura Ingalls Wilder books, think it goes back to the 19th century when families like Charles Ingalls' were vulnerable only to the weather. "Pa" Ingalls depended on other people for very few things. Nails, cornmeal, gunpowder and a small amount of lead were about all he ever needed to purchase. He didn't need to buy water, food, electricity or fuel. All he needed he could create with a few tools. All his vital possessions could be loaded into a wagon. He had mastered the information he needed to be independent and free.

Of course, the answer for civilization is not that everyone live like pioneer homesteaders. But the answer for people who wish to survive the worst of the y2k dangers is that they may have to live non vulnerable lives for a few short years -- and their lifestyles might look very much like Pa Ingalls'.

It is my prayer that the problems are not so severe that they could cause real starvation, riots, and strict government interventions like martial law.

But this book will be frank about the worst that could come. In May, 1998, *New York Post* reporter Niles Lathem asked Y2k experts what they thought life would be like in the first hours of the year 2000. He spoke to Sen. Bob Bennett (R-Utah) and Rep. Stephen Horn (R-Calif.) (who chair special congressional panels on the Year 2000 problem), Councilman Andrew Eristoff (R-Manhattan) who is monitoring the city's readiness, Canadian cyberscholar and lecturer Peter deJager, Lou Marcoccio, research director of the Gartner Group, which is consulting with Fortune 500 companies on the issue, and Michael Higgins, president of Century Services, which is installing software for companies to make their computer systems Year 2000 compliant.

These experts provided fictional scenarios, but they are educated fictional scenarios. Some of them look like this: At 12:00:30 a.m. the power grid for Manhattan goes out. Three seconds later Times Square goes dark. Twelve seconds later the radar goes out at Kennedy Airport and an incoming 737 disappears off the air traffic controller's screen. Meanwhile, in Russia, alarms are going off at a Nuclear Power plant just nine hours after the date rollover.

At Fort Meade, the National Security Agency, an Air Force captain discovers that Communications between Iraqi National Guard commanders in Basra and Baghdad become gibberish. The NSA has lost vital code-breaking code.

At 8:01 a.m., Columbia Presbyterian Medical Center, Manhattan, the internal clock in the admitting office's computer system has changed the year from 1999 to 1900 - which means all patient records are lost and the hospital cannot access or record medical histories and insurance information. Harried administrators spend the night turning away patients or making them wait. The chief resident spots emergency patients lying on gurneys in a hallway and demands that they be treated no matter what the problems with processing. Angry clerks prepare admissions forms by hand. Billing is a nightmare that will just have to wait.

The MRI, CT Scan and IV machines appear to be working. But in the average hospital, there are 29 mission-critical systems and more than 15,000 medical devices that depend on computers. And that doesn't include the 5,000 personal computers and computers that control the hospital infrastructure, which is entirely dependent on electricity.

It will be months before all the problems are identified. At 8:02 a.m., Kennedy Airport, chaos reigns.

At 2:00 p.m., Attica State Prison, Attica, N.Y., a near-riot has just been quelled in Cell Block D of this maximum security prison. The computer system that controls rows of cells opened the doors an hour early and it took three hours for guards to restore order. Upstairs, an associate warden is trying to put out another fire. On his desk are 1,575 release orders for hardened criminals - all of whom are supposed to serve lengthy sentences. The reason for the mixup: an 00-related glitch in the clock in the prison computer that made them eligible for release. 6:00 a.m. EST - General Motors Plant A, Detroit. Managers send workers home. The production line isn't functioning. Despite $500 million spent to make all factories and labs Year 2000 compliant, half the robotic devices at the plant won't turn on and there are problems with the computerized metal cutters. There's word that another plant didn't open because no one could get inside - the dreaded 00 sent security systems haywire.

Could scenarios like these really happen? Yes. Not one is an exaggeration of the evidence seen by the experts who made these fictional projections.

PREFACE

What <u>Could</u> Become Of Us?

"We can only conclude that it is too much to ask of us poor twentieth-century humans to think, to believe, to grasp the possibility that the system might fail...we cannot grasp the simple and elementary fact that this technology can blow a fuse."

Obscure British sociologist after the
1965 power blackout in New York City

Before he was Speaker of the U.S. House of Representatives, history professor Newton Leroy Gingrich, Ph.D., could be heard describing the history of civilization in three important "waves." The First Wave was said to be primitive family hunting and family farming. The Second Wave was the remarkable industrial revolution, which truly revolutionized the world with machines, factories, new family structures and new government structures. The pinnacle of the Second Wave occurred at the beginning of the 20th century. Understandably, there was much pride in man's technological accomplishments. One crowning symbol of these mental evolutionary achievements was the 1913 launching of the "completely unsinkable" *R.M.S. Titanic*, a masterpiece of technological perfection.

The Third Wave, which began in earnest after WWII, is said to be the modern information society with its automated living, computerized business functions and specialized intellectual elite (sometimes called "the brain lords").

In every instance in which I have heard this phrase used, the "Third Wave" is spoken of with near-reverential awe. It is inferred that computer power has brought man to new heights of technological perfection, individual autonomy and humanistic potential. High-tech discoveries are supposed to stand as monuments to man's powers of self-directed, upward intellectual evolution and unlimited future potential.

Indeed, computers are pretty impressive. And it is thrilling to see the explosion of technological marvels. And it is enjoyable to experience the ways this technology makes our lives easier and more exciting.

But what will future historians say about today's impressive Third Wave?

Was it the door through which men passed on their way to true technological perfection? Was it the dawn of an age in which man realized his true mental powers and ultimate human potential?

Here's what I believe will be recorded about our impressive Third Wave: *It was the brief moment in human civilization in which men were at their most vulnerable, and suffered for that vulnerability.*

In the early 1970s, Oxford historian James Burke began to realize this and made some interesting comments on the BBC in 1977. In telling the story about the 1965 electrical power blackout in New York, he reminds us that "one small malfunction can cripple the entire system." And he doesn't just mean New York power. He means the entire system of technology to which most of us have entrusted our lives.

The 1965 blackout is instructive. At 5:16PM November 9, the power went off. An estimated 800,000 people were trapped in the subways. Only half of the hospitals had auxiliary power. The 250 flights en route to JFK airport had to be diverted. One of them was on its final approach to landing when the lights on the runway went out, and all communication with the control tower ceased. Elevators stopped. Water supplies dried up. Massive traffic jams choked the streets as traffic lights went out. All street lights went dark. 80,000 square miles of the richest, most highly industrialized areas of Western civilization came to a virtual standstill.

Burke finds it interesting that the reaction of the New Yorkers was to assume that the power would come back on instantly. When it didn't, they assumed it would come on in a few minutes. He said it would have been unthinkable to contemplate more than a momentary outage.

"The modern city-dweller," reported Burke, "cannot permit himself to think that his ability to cope in such a situation is in doubt. If he did so he would be forced to accept the uncertainty of his position, because once the meager reserves of food and light and warmth have been exhausted, what then?"

Indeed, what then? In this book, we want to raise that question about the y2k challenge. If the disruptions to our computers last more than a moment, *What Then?* If our present meager reserves of food and light and warmth are wiped out by y2k, *What Then?*

This book does not have an anti-progress or an anti-technology bias. The authors like both progress and technology. They are devoting a lot of time to the effort of planning a new expansion of technology and progress after the y2k bug destroys some of our present technology.

But how do we prepare for the inconvenience of its first assault on our lives? We are vulnerable because our entire society is dependent and interdependent on computers. What *could* happen to us? Could the power black out and stay out for ten hours? Ten days? Ten years? The answer to all of the above is, Yes. There is a y2k scenario in which 98% of the world's cities lose power for ten years. What would that be like?

We can visualize the aftermath of warfare and hurricanes, because we have seen ugly photographs. Usually we don't look at those pictures long, because they are depressing. Most people quickly shift their attention to something more pleasant to look at.

But it's time to try to picture a peacetime calamity that touches every home, including yours. Exactly what would the y2k crisis look like? Even a short version. How bad could it be if it lasts longer than "momentary?" If it lasts longer than a month or two, what will become of your job, your money, your neighborhood, and your future?

Try to imagine this likely scenario without putting this book down:

If a nationwide panic doesn't begin before January 1, 2000, then the y2k crisis will get underway in wintertime. We will realize just how seriously we depended on computers we never saw, or never knew existed. Winter isn't a good time for a crisis. Panic will begin rising on January 2. By Monday, January 3, the crisis could have touched everyone in America. By January 10, panic could be serious, and it could be everywhere. Not just because electrical power and phone service is intermittent, but because people will finally start realizing that the crisis could last a while and that they are not prepared for it.

At the time this book is being sent to the press, there is no evidence that by January 15, 2000, electrical power will be back up and functioning, no evidence that fresh water will be available, no evidence that banks will be open, no evidence that businesses will be able to function without banking, or that trains and trucks will be able to move food from rural to urban areas. It also appears that airlines may not be running after the self imposed shutdown New Year's period. Perhaps a few cargo planes would be allowed to fly, but commercial passenger traffic may be considered too dangerous.

It sounds almost criminal to even suggest such a scenario. If you read carefully, you'll see that the editors of this book are not announcing such terrible scenarios. We are pointing out that there is no evidence to suggest that these bad scenarios will <u>not</u> happen. We're not saying they will happen. We're saying that <u>all</u> the available evidence points to a dangerous likelihood that the services we take for granted will fail. There is no technological evidence to the contrary. Then we try to take the responsible position of considering what this means. Few people allow themselves to take this next step in their thinking. What does a failure of services mean? Honestly. It means that for almost all of us our occupations could suddenly vanish, our homes could become damaged or obsolete and that every urban grocery store could be empty.

It means that phone service, police protection, mail service and medical services, like trips to the dentist to fix a toothache, could not be available. It means our toilets could not be working, our pipes possibly frozen and broken (and waiting to flood our property if the water comes back on), and that hungry people could be sniffing around the neighborhood to see who might have any food stored away somewhere.

If trucks are not running, then the filling stations will be out of fuel. Those cars that will run (a percentage of cars built after 1981 will not run), will probably be clogging the highways leading from the cities, as families flee metropolitan areas by the tens of thousands.

This picture looks like the end of the world. But it's not. Every western nation should be able to rebuild an orderly society. The issue this book attempts to address is, *what will become of you and your family before that society is rebuilt?*

People who are *prepared* for a modern crisis can be living calmly and safely without electricity, jobs, phones, money, grocery stores and even dentists. They can be living without panic. Most of the folks who began preparing for y2k in the spring of 1997 were considered a bit kooky by the rest of us. By early 1998 there were thousands of kooks who didn't care if anyone thought they were kooky. They cared about what might happen to their families, and they started looking reality squarely in the eye.

They were wise. They knew their emergency lifestyle would not be easy, but they knew it would beat the alternatives. The key word for all of us is *preparation*. The better prepared a family is, the easier and more enjoyable is the alternative lifestyle.

During war and natural disasters, almost no one is prepared, because almost everyone is caught off guard. For the y2k crisis, the date for the trouble is set on the calendar.

If you are reading this book ahead of the crisis, you are at a great advantage. This book will show you how to responsibly do four things:

How to face the facts about y2k.

There will be a disruption of our modern lifestyle. No one knows how long it will last, but experts now know it will hit us in late 1999, and hit very hard on January 1, 2000. Government bureaucrats will do everything they must do, including lying, to avert panic, but the truth is that y2k will hurt.

How to mentally consider long term hardship and how you can overcome it with the resources you now possess.

You may not have a lot. If you're like most Americans, you're living from paycheck to paycheck, and the possessions you now own are playthings. But you probably have enough assets to survive.

How to convert some of your playthings into wealth.

In other words, it's time to sell some of your stuff that will be worthless, and buy some stuff that will be priceless.

How to decide what to buy

It's not easy figuring out what possessions are priority possessions. This book will try to demonstrate the relative value of things we have never considered valuable, like,

food with a shelf life

water purification gear

long-term supplies of medicine

geographic safety

alternative power sources

family protection weapons

reliable transportation

This book will also help you anticipate what secondary possessions it would be good to have "stockpiled." This word has come into disfavor in the late 1990s. Some people with political agendas have tried to associate that word with aggressive military tyrants or apocalyptic cult leaders. Others who misuse the word suggest that our society and government must be trusted to continually provide constant gratification and the uninterrupted supply of every convenience. Stockpiling is nothing more than acquiring the things you need that may not be available anywhere but in your pile of stock. Hoarding, on the other hand, is deliberately taking more than you need and withholding it from the needy. If you truly and legitimately might need it, you're not hoarding, you're stockpiling. Stockpiling is the ethical thing to do in the situation you are now facing. If you want to make sure you're not a hoarder, stockpile a little extra for you neighbors who were not as wise as you were.

Before the days of supermarkets and the one-shelf-pantries of our suburban homes, everyone stockpiled. Our grandparents, for example, knew they would not have food through the winter unless they grew it, harvested it and stockpiled it. Because it's impossible to stockpile everything we could possibly need, it is wise to have extra items that can be readily traded to others who may have those things we failed to put back. This book will try to identify a few of the more potentially valuable year 2000 "extras," like:

> gold
> silver
> platinum
> US clad coins
> toilet paper
> coffee
> common ammunition
> cigarettes
> soap
> medicine
> nails
> salt
> small tools

What the y2k crisis is beginning to show us is that we late 20th-Century moderns have made ourselves very comfortable, and somewhat lazy, in a world that has become our playground. If we can make ourselves comfortable with tools instead of toys, and with constructive work instead of unconstructive frolicking, then someday we will look back on this y2k surprise as the best thing that ever happened to us.

This book will be most valuable before the year 2000. In fact, our research indicates that many products and services listed in this book will not be available by phone or mail after October, 1999. That same research indicates that you and your community can not depend on government help, The National Guard, The Red Cross, or any other bureaucratic agency in the first two years after 2000. Read through this book immediately and figure out the strategy that will make you less vulnerable. If you are able to act on the suggestions in this book, you can actually be self-sufficient, and not dependent on any of the technology that may be affected by the y2k crisis.

In 1977 James Burke said it was a myth that today's dependent urbanites could live independent of technology. He's only right if we stay as ignorant as we are at this moment, and as vulnerable as we are at this moment. Most of us would undoubtedly remain this ignorant if we didn't have this special motivation: Thousands of computer experts are pointing to a specific day on the calendar, waving their arms, trying to get our attention so that we understand we can no longer depend on our computer technology on that date. If we act immediately, their fair warning gives us time to change our ignorance into preparedness, and to turn myth into lifesaving reality.

CHAPTER 1
What Does the Millennium Bug Look Like?

"It's ugly. The problem's going to be pretty bad."

Andrew Grove
CEO, Intel Corp.
April 24, 1998

The millennium bug is sneaky. It's lying in ambush in computer code. It's hiding in tiny chips we cannot look into. And it's waiting to claim credit for problems it doesn't directly cause. We've seen little parts of the millennium bug, but it won't show us much else until December 31, 1999, when it will jump out at us saying, "gotcha!"

That's when we'll know what the bug looks like - when we see what it does to us at midnight, December 31, 1999. Until then, we can only make a limited diagnosis, and that's what makes the y2k threat a very uncomfortable unknown. The world's greatest experts on the problem are genuinely unsure of what will happen. But all of them share very grave concerns. At press time, they agree that there will be many disruptions and failures of hardware and software at midnight, December 31, 1999, and many more beyond that date.

Some of those failures will inconvenience us two or three

days. Others could be catastrophic, like an uncontained failure of electrical power. If smaller failures can be contained, and if some backup or manual solution is readily available to fall back on, America can live with those temporary aggravations. Each one will be rather maddening because they will be very frustrating inconveniences, like, for example, the Teamsters' strike on UPS in August 1997. That inconvenience was not caused by computer failure but, all the same, we lost one of those conveniences America takes for granted. We coped with it because it was temporary, and because the alternative delivery systems were kept up and running.

By themselves, y2k inconveniences like brief banking disruptions, the loss of electrical power for a few hours, the shutting off of our water supply for perhaps a day, a week-long delay in receiving a social security check, probably won't threaten our safety.

Unfortunately, it will become clear in 1999 that the millennium bug is somewhat incapable of causing small, brief disruptions. By definition, it is like the Hydra: it's a monster with vicious new heads that appear with every effort to strike it down. Y2k becomes especially dangerous when a computer failure becomes a trigger effect, starting a series of ripple effects that can dangerously affect the safety of anyone who is not prepared for sudden and prolonged hardship. The worst ripples will be hardware ripples. For example, a two minute electrical brownout might damage some power plant hardware that may take months to replace, and months to test before it can be turned on again. If it can be turned on again.

Software ripples could last as long or longer. The UPS strike triggered consequences that affected the jobs of over 15,000 workers long after the strike was over. An even better example is

26

the 17-day strike at two Dayton, Ohio brake plants in March of 1996. In just 17 days, the absence of those brake parts triggered the shut down of 26 of 29 GM plants in North America, as well as 18 other parts plants. More than 177,000 workers were furloughed. It also stopped work at countless other suppliers and services, and cost GM about $900 million.

The strike was, of course, a political shut-down of the plant. We should study it because software failures could shut it down just as tightly on January 1, 2000. That 17-day shut-down of two small Ohio companies proves that the ripple effect can go far and deep. What will happen if the economy stays up and the millennium bug shuts down even two companies for 17 days? 17 weeks? Or 17 months?

With each computer disruption, the managers of every system affected will try to contain the disorders so that not too many ripples begin to spread. But the more significant failures could create inconveniences for periods of weeks, months and years. They might last that long because tiny ripple effects have ways of turning into tidal waves.

Exactly what causes the small disruptions? Back in the early days of computer programming, many computer programs were coded to accept only two digits as a year indicator (i.e. mm/dd/yy). The century, "19", has always been implied. Computer space was expensive back then, and programmers could save millions of dollars per megabyte if they could scrimp on two digits. "19" were to easiest two digits to get rid of, and it is estimated that this economizing of digits saved some $36 billion.

Following timid celebrations New Year's Eve 1999, calendars, computers and microprocessors around the world will roll over to 01/01/00. And when that change occurs, every home, business, and government agency will be affected to one degree or another.

    As expert Rick Cowles respectfully points out, computers are basically stupid. They follow sets of instructions that humans program them to do. When those instructions make no sense to the computer, strange things can happen. Maybe the program will run erroneously, or perhaps even cease to run. This is the Millennium Bug. It's like a virus that causes insanity. Infected with this virus, our poor, stupid computers go insane trying to figure out the stupid instructions given them by nearsighted programmers.

CHAPTER 2
What Other Calamities Teach Us

*"There is no danger that the
Titanic will sink. The boat is unsinkable
and nothing but inconvenience will be
suffered by the passengers."*

> Philip Franklin, April 15, 1912
> Vice President, White Star Line,
> Commenting on radio messages that the Titanic
> might be in distress. The ship was, in fact, lying
> at the bottom of the North Atlantic.

The hardship of America's Great Depression and Dust Bowl years is still vivid with many survivors. But it is rarely discussed and even more rarely assumed that similar hardships could be experienced again in such a modern society.

In 1936 a young reporter named John Steinbeck visited a California labor camp populated by refugee families who had left homes in the Midwest. He saw starvation, disease and despair "everywhere." Children and adults were dying from lack of food and clean water.

The y2k threat could pose more serious dangers to the US than were seen in the Great Depression of the early 1930s. Why? Because the disappearance of critical goods and services could happen suddenly. In the Great Depression it happened gradually.

Today's public's response could be uncivil and uncontrolled. In the Great Depression, Americans behaved themselves responsibly, for the most part. Our grandparents had a built-in work ethic, a neighborliness ethic, and a survival ethic that later generations appear to have lost.

The Great Depression is called "Great" primarily because it lasted a long time. The weak economy hammered individual families lower and lower, year after year. Peggy Terry, a survivor, remembers a visit she made to Oklahoma City: "Here were all these people living in old rusted-out car bodies....One family...was living in a piano box. This wasn't just a little section, this was maybe ten miles wide and ten miles long. People living in whatever they could junk together."

My Grandmother organized classes for women teaching them how to economize on food and shelter. She taught them how to make underwear from gunny sacks and how to make clothing from automobile seat covers. It's been a long time since Americans had to live through an extended crisis. How would we handle it? A few of us do pretty well when we are notified of a coming hurricane, snow storm, or flood. And the younger generation, even Generation-X-ers, have been known to pull together rather nobly in times of weather emergencies. But what about a crisis that may hit harder than a storm, or may last longer than the effects of a flood?

Last winter, some of our neighbors were caught unprepared for an electrical blackout when a careless construction crew cut through a major power artery. Outside temperatures were dropping toward zero and our neighbors had no flashlights, candles, matches, and no way to keep warm except their electric heat source, which was dead and cold. They were grossly unprepared, and they suffered.

When power came on 12 hours later our neighbors didn't blame themselves for their shortsightedness. They blamed and cursed "the government." In fact, they are still grumbling about how the the government let them down.

Those neighbors, like most of us, are spoiled. True, they were inconvenienced, and they were cold, and they were in some real danger. But they have never seen real hardship. They have been taught that the government will always make life easy, and they have believed it. They have seen the government intervene when they personally needed financial subsidies of one kind or another, and they have seen the government extend its control over almost every segment of society. They are certainly not alone in believing that "everybody is entitled to constant uninterrupted government care," and they expect that care to come with no risks, no dangers, no hardships, no worries and, certainly, no disappointments.

True, the government is bigger than ever. Its agents often boast about its modern abilities. But responsible American families must admit that the ultimate responsibility for survival does not rest with the government. It rests with families. It rests with the head of each household. History teaches that households which survive periods of hardship do it without reliance on anyone but themselves and without any support but what they prepared ahead of time and what a close group of neighbors prepare after the crisis begins.

The modern twentieth century has been a century of increasing government power and sophistication. Many governments have done marvelous things, but all of them have been powerless to stop some of history's worst calamities. Millions of people have died in the twentieth century because of the failure of good governments. In many other cases, hundreds

of millions have died because of the successes of bad governments.

The survivors of national calamities were always people who prepared themselves for specific hardships before they happened. In the coming y2k calamity, no one should make the mistake of thinking that the government will be ready and able to help. *It will not be there to lean on.* The government's computers are in terrible shape. In May 1997 the Federal Government OMB report says: "Unless they are fixed or replaced, [computers] will fail at the turn of the century in one of three ways: they will reject legitimate entries, or they will compute erroneous results, or they will simply not run."

Add to this the statement in the February, 1977, report by the General Accounting Office in its report, "Year 2000 Computing Crisis: An Assessment Guide": "Every federal agency is at risk of widespread systems failures".

The government itself will have a tough time surviving. Computer programmer and author Ed Yourdon says it won't. "Period."

Time Magazine, June 15, 1998, put it well. "John Koskinen is in charge of making sure the U.S. government's computers don't crash come Jan. 1, 2000. Koskinen's task is not just daunting; it's impossible."

Representative Stephen Horn, R-CA, Chairman of the House Subcommittee on Government Management, Information, and Technology, has been grading government agencies on their y2k repair progress. Part of his May, 1998 report included the following:

"About two weeks ago, a single communications satellite spun out of control. For the next couple of days, 90 percent of all pagers in the United States were useless, many television stations

had nothing to broadcast, several news wires failed, and gasoline stations, banks, and retail stores that use small satellite dishes found themselves in the dark. All this resulted from the failure of just one satellite. It was a timely reminder of what is really at stake in the smooth functioning of technology—a tiny hint of what the Year 2000 could bring. With Federal Y2K efforts cast in this urgent light, we turn to the latest data on Federal preparations.

"Overall, the Federal Government earned an 'F.' Underlying this dismal grade is a disturbing slow-down in the Government's rate of progress. For the quarter ending February 15, the Government brought mission-critical systems into compliance at a rate of 9.4 percent; for the quarter that ended May 15, the rate of progress slowed to 7.9 percent. This would be discouraging in any context. Less than a year before the March 1999 deadline for Y2K repairs, a reduction in productivity is deeply troubling. This trend must be reversed.

"Specific agency grades raise further concerns. The Department of Defense earned a 'D' and is still not on track to complete Y2K compliance efforts until two years after the date change. "The Department of Transportation merited an 'F.' This grade includes the Federal Aviation Administration, which provides crucial services to the flying public. Without dramatic improvements, the Nation's air traffic could face serious disruptions for an extended period after December 31, 1999. The Department of Health and Human Services also earned an 'F.' The Medicare program, among others, depends on the smooth functioning of its computer systems."

Mr. Horn noted that The Social Security Administration seems to be on track, but that all their good work may be for naught if the Treasury Department's Financial Management Service (FMS) fails to get on the ball. The FMS is the agency that

actually writes the Social Security checks that go out, and is far from ready.

If Americans could be persuaded that the government cannot help, will they help themselves? History shows us that, even with warning, most people don't act to prepare for a problem, they wait until the last minute and then try to flee the problem, and often the problem overtakes them. A recent study by the U.S. Navy revealed that many Navy airmen died needlessly in damaged planes because they would not bail out. The study concluded that these airmen preferred the familiarity of the cockpit to the relative unfamiliarity of the parachute landing site. This is precisely why most of us are reluctant to take unfamiliar steps to protect ourselves when we are perfectly comfortable at home.

The situation along the Mississippi in 1878 has a lesson for us. There was an epidemic of Yellow Fever. Scientists didn't know what carried the sickness, but they knew it was coming north. They could track it, and they could predict when it was going to hit Memphis. The media tried to paint a picture that everything would be just fine. People should have left town, but no newspaper was recommending such drastic action.

Then, quite predictably, just as the disease was due to hit the city, a man caught the disease and died down by the wharf. At that moment, people accepted reality. In the next ten days, 55% of the population fled the city. Those who stayed were in tough shape. All the policemen who stayed died. All Caucasians who stayed caught the plague and two thirds of them died. Those who escaped in time lived.

This book was written to help American families begin to understand the responsibilities they need to take on themselves, to point out twelve possible hardships that may be caused by the y2k

computer problem, and to offer preliminary suggestions on preparing for those specific hardships.

Scientists can look back on the Yellow Fever plague and say, "Mosquitoes carried it." I believe future scientists will look back on the Y2K plague and say, "It's quite simple and understandable why civilization crashed. The society was too computer interdependent and the computer software and hardware was not designed to work in the year 2000. The problem was so simple and easily fixable, and people had so much confidence in computer science, that the possibility of a crash could not be mentally accepted. They ignored that possibility at their peril. They put off the repair effort believing that technology would provide a last minute solution. When no solution came, the technology crashed. Those who were not prepared for non-technological life crashed also."

Here I must digress and say something about the U.S. Military. Many Americans served in the military when it was a proud, professional institution. In spite of its bureaucratic mass, it could get things done and hold its own as the world's number one superpower. For this reason it is hard for many veterans or others to imagine that y2k could sneak up on our military. The military is seen as the high-tech embodiment of the US government, and will be as unfazed as it was in Desert Storm.

As long as the military is seen as untouchable by the millennium bug, I'm afraid a lot of people will continue to put their trust in the continuity of the US government. That's why I must point out that y2k has ambushed the strongest military in the world. Neither the American people nor our allies can lean on the US military. It will be defeated by y2k.

If you think it is frightening and possibly destabilizing to have this kind of information get out, you're right. The National

Security Agency just decided that information about the Pentagon's lack of progress in dealing with y2k must now be classified, according to the May 18, 1998 *Federal Computer Week* .

Said the article, "NSA has determined that all information detailing DOD's computers and its efforts to fix the Year 2000 problem are a "national security interest" and "highly sensitive." As a result, the Pentagon has cut off the military services and DOD project offices from the Defense Integrated Support Tool (DIST) database, which the Defense Information Systems Agency maintains to provide details on all DOD computer systems and interfaces for use in planning and deployment. . . .

"DOD began using DIST to track Year 2000 compliance in August 1996, and a Dec. 19,1997, memo from the Office of the Secretary of Defense to DOD chief information officers identified DIST as the "central, authoritative database for tracking resolution of the Year 2000-related problems for systems throughout the department."

"That aggregation of extensive details about Year 2000 problems with DOD systems poses a threat to national security, according to NSA.

"'The DOD's Y2K conversion effort is a national security interest,' NSA reported in a statement supplied to FCW. 'All information detailing these information systems and the progress being made toward their conversions is considered to be highly sensitive.'"

"...One former high-ranking DOD official described the classification issue as symptomatic of what he called the Pentagon's "gross mismanagement" of Year 2000 issues. . . ."

Before the NSA threw the security blanket over this sensitive information, what reports were getting out about y2k repair?

Earlier in 1998, Bill Dates, Army Y2K Program Manager, sent an e-mail to Dr. Gary North to correct a small error in Dr. North's figures. Wrote Dates, "[You're] close but not exactly correct. The number of 209,204 should be 209,042 and represents the number of systems and devices in the Army that need to be fixed from a Y2K perspective. This total includes information systems, weapons systems, PCs, servers, communications hubs and routers, telephone switches, heating and air conditioning systems, elevators, etc. The number represents the total estimate of all things that need to be fixed (both large and small) in the Army as of January 1998. It includes much more than what are generally classified as "systems"."

209,042 is a big number, especially when the year is 1998 and repair on many of these has not even started. A congressional aide told me that the Pentagon was not even certain which systems were critical, and did not know if all departments were sure how many computer systems were under their authority. It was the aide's opinion that the Pentagon was ignorant about three things: how many systems required fixing, how to fix the systems they knew about, and how long it would take. He said the published estimates about where the military stands are far, far from the reality.

So what is the the real story on the most powerful military in the world. Does anyone know? The congressional aide says some of the programmers deep in the Pentagon basement know. "But our superiors are afraid to pass the word up the chain," the aide has been told by these programmers. The message they are eager to pass up the chain is largely one big military expletive which, translated, means, "We're sunk."

One public estimate by an auditing agency projected the Pentagon's y2k repairs to be completed more than a decade too late. What would happen to an America that had to go without a military for ten years?

In 1997, American Scientist magazine reported on a number of potential military computer failures and noted that "Worst of all, defense systems could cease to protect our country from potential invaders. Consider, for example, that satellites of the Global Positioning System keep track of the date by counting the weeks since Jan. 6, 1980."

"The count is maintained as a 10-bit value," the American Scientist article reported. "Thus, it has a maximum range of 1,024 weeks." In August 1999, the counter will roll over, and GPS receivers will read it as 1980." This is extremely serious because so many military functions are tied to the GPS system. For that matter, so are many banking and other vital civilian functions of society. Some of the world's more important financial transactions are registered and timed by the same GPS clocks.

According to a study by Congress's General Accounting Office and summarized by the Center for Security Policy, the Federal Aviation Administration was found to be far behind in their y2k efforts. The study then asks, "Is the Pentagon in Any Better Shape? Unfortunately, there is reason to believe that the armed forces are no more prepared than the FAA to deal with the implications of the Millennium Bug.

"The Air Force estimates there are 2,944 automated information systems and weapons embedded systems in its inventory and that the majority of these systems will have to be either renovated, replaced, or retired before 1 January 2000. Of the 2,944 systems, 550 (about 19 percent) are considered to be mission-critical systems, that is, they directly support wartime operations."

In a story related by Peter DeJager, one 1998 missile test

demonstrated the potential problems with Air Force embedded systems. The test missile was fired, and then its computers were directed to roll over to January 1, 2000. The rollover caused the on-board systems to fail, and the missile did a U-turn, heading back toward the launching pad. Fortunately, the Air Force had anticipated failure, and an airborne fighter was able to shoot the missile out of the sky before it blew up the launch area.

On June 21, 1998 *The Boston Globe* reported that the military tested the underground NORAD computers for y2k and the system crashed. According to a spokesman for the Mitre Corporation, the system that controls American's nuclear arsenal froze up at the stroke of midnight.

In testimony to the Senate Armed Services Committee, Assistant Secretary of Defense John Hamre said, "Despite [y2k repair] efforts... there is no guarantee all DOD systems will be free of risk by the immovable deadline of January 1, 2000. Systems whose risks have been mitigated through renovation and testing could fail, and the failure of one system could disrupt many others."

A CNN news reporter has become concerned that this kind of disruption might affect the launching software of nuclear weapons. He's having a hard time getting accurate information from the Pentagon. On June 14, 1998 he interviewed John Pike of the of the Federation of American Scientists, who said, "There's a real risk though that we could see the sort of computer malfunctions that we've seen in previous years, where the command and control systems erroneously report that an attack is in progress; erroneously direct missiles to shoot at the wrong target; and at a minimum, cause all of the countries to put their missiles on much higher levels of alert, because they're concerned about their unreliable warning systems.

"So, in all probability, nothing is going to happen, but there is a small, finite risk that this could lead to an accidental nuclear war, simply because people fail to fix their computers. And that's obviously a totally unacceptable risk. . . . What we have not seen is an evaluation of the nuclear command and control systems, the intelligence systems. And, in fact, the National Security Agency is starting to classify a lot of this information under the theory that these are just not going to be fixed, and we need to start hiding that vulnerability. So clearly, a lot of these things are not going to be fixed in time."

If US missiles are vulnerable, what about Russian and Chinese systems, built largely from stolen American technology? Computer programmer Chuck Missler has pointed out that the Russians and Chinese could not fix these systems because they didn't steal the source code of the software, just the business-end of the software. Could their confused systems accidentally launch against the US?

"[T]heir early warning system is fragile," Assistant Secretary of Defense John Hamre said in a presentation to congress.

According to Reuters, Russian forces lacked a program to deal with the Y2K problem--the inability of many computers to interpret correctly the century that dawns in 18 months. . . .

"Although the Cold War has been over for years," reported Reuters, "the United States and Russia each still keep ready to deliver on short notice roughly 2,500 nuclear-tipped weapons on missiles, bombers, and submarines. . . .

"Calling the Y2K glitch the electronic equivalent of El Niño weather pattern, Hamre said: 'This is going to have implications in the world and in American society we can't even comprehend.'

"I will be first to say we're not going to be without some nasty surprises," he said.

On June 4, 1998, the *Netly News* reported, "Of all the federal agencies bumbling through Y2K fixes, the Department of Defense is in particularly poor health. Repairs of the most vital computer systems were just 9 percent complete as of this spring -- though the Pentagon began Y2K planning in 1995. More optimistic projections predict the Defense Department will finish its Y2K work in 2002. . .

"About 120 of the Army's 376 most vital information and weapons systems need to be fixed and have not been revamped yet. Worse yet, 17,000 of 88,000 military communications systems aren't century-savvy (and 18,000 still have to be tested)."

Because y2k progress is now a classified topic, Americans may not hear exactly how weak our military is. Will many continue to think the US government can do miracles, and lean heavily on the government to prevent any prolonged hardship?

Will the crash on January 1, 2000 be Doomsday? The proverbial Doomsday is usually thought to be death and destruction for everyone. I believe y2k will be death and destruction for only some people. Others will live through the crisis and begin the rebuilding process.

In 1936, when John Steinbeck visited that Labor Camp in California, he observed that it was a place of despair in which families who had escaped the desolation of their home towns were dying in obscurity and squalor 1000 miles from home. It looked hopeless. It looked like Doomsday.

But a man named Leo Hart had a vision to build a school in that camp so as to give the families some stability, some education, and a future.

The county government would not help or cooperate, but Leo Hart collected enough scrap lumber, sewer pipe, volunteer teachers and food supplies, and he built that school into the best school in the county. The refugees who were once ridiculed and despised by Californians were soon envied. It soon became clear that they had the hope, the confidence and the tools they needed to help rebuild a hurting culture. It was not long before most of that county's California parents wanted to send their children to the labor camp school.

If Leo Hart had not taken the effort to rebuild where he could, those families would have been decimated. Survivors would have turned to crime, or would have continued wandering aimlessly as defeated, suffering refugees.

If we focus on rebuilding after the y2k crash, our present course of action becomes much more clear: we need to order our affairs so we can survive with enough resources and strength to begin the rebuilding process. We must not lean on anyone else, especially the government, but we must be ready to let those who are weaker lean on us.

CHAPTER 3
What Will Become of Your Home?

"You can't call 911 if there is no dial tone..."

Cliff Kurtzman
The Tenagra Corp

*"Be very careful about where you live
and who your neighbors are.
It could be a life and death choice once the fur flies."*

Open Forum,   www.trappped.com

*"The only thing worse than leaving your home
is wishing you had left your home."*

Julian Gregori

Let me come straight to a critical point. If any of the computer problems cause urban chaos which lasts more than four days, personal safety will be of bigger concern in our cities than any other y2k problem discussed in this book. It is my opinion that there will be serious city disruptions that last much longer than four years, making life in the city impractical for any except the most hard-core urban survivalist. Cities are now so structured

43

that they can't function without electricity or without functioning computers. Damaged power plants will try get back up and running as soon as they can, and they will make delivery of power to urban areas a priority, but they cannot now guarantee that they will be operating at all in 2000 or 2001. Non-functioning cities, if inhabited, will be chaotic. Because urban chaos can be deadly to innocent bystanders, every urban family needs alternative housing -- at least 100 miles outside any city over 100,000 population. Even farther would be better. The safest bottom line solution to the y2k threat appears to be 'get out of town before the computers go down.'

When people are confronted with facts about y2k disruptions, they usually respond with one of two attitudes: responsible reflection or kneejerk denial. Those in the former category usually fall further into categories of *students* or *non-students*. The non-students seem to know they will need to do something, and wait for the students to tell them what to do. What I find interesting about the non-students is their reluctance to think the problem through. They know there is a problem, but they will not allow themselves to cogitate on what that means. Students, on the other hand, are not only gathering additional information, they are *thinking* about the implications of the problem. Few people do this. Few people try to imagine what it would truly be like if their pantries were empty, their water shut off, and no food in the grocery store. Thinking students who once thought they could not possibly move suddenly understand that they could be forced to move if there was no food or water.

(Incidentally, this is the definition of a refugee. A refugee is someone who is forced to move at an inconvenient time. Most refugees wander because they did not make earlier arrangements to move when it would have been more convenient.)

Typically, within a month of industrious study, even the most skeptical of students realize that they need to take a specific course of action. Their first actions classify them either as *urban survivalists* or *rural survivalists.* I'm sure almost all of them would object to the 'survivalist' label, but it is clear from their own actions that they picture certain urban scenarios they want to survive.

Most urban survivalists admit that their chances of survival would be better in the country, but are staying because of responsibilities they feel to family members who are in denial and won't move, or to the ignorant masses who will need material or spiritual charity.

I believe denialist family members may move out of the city very abruptly in August or September, 1999 as certain events or media coverage push them into the category of rural survivalist virtually overnight.

As for those city dwellers who remain in ignorance or denial right up until the deadline, the opportunity to provide charity to them may be very temporary and highly risky. Here's why:

The voluntary evacuation of America's largest cities is expected to begin in earnest on Monday, January 3, 2000. Not only will apartments empty out, but also single-family homes.

The migration of refugees will not be an orderly event.

I know a nice lady who understands that the situation could be desperate. She is planning to stay in the city to see whom she can help. I'm afraid she will discover that it's nearly impossible to help a stampeding herd, and completely impossible to help the ghosts of a ghost town.

An interesting strategy of another urban survivalist is to hide his family (and three years' supplies) in the city -- in a camouflaged building -- a building that looks burned out, boarded up and empty. After the throngs leave, he believes it will be safer to be in an empty city than in in the country where the gleaning process begins to take on criminal proportions.

Rural survivalists, of course, are planning to move out of the city early, and get more than 200 miles away. I believe all of these concerned survivalists are right to expect lengthy periods of disorder in the countryside within 200 miles of the big metro areas.

What should you do? Is there a right approach and a wrong approach?

Some church leaders have criticized rural survivalists who have made the decision to "cut and run." Have those families cut and run? Or have they moved to new places where they will find new opportunities to help others?

I believe church leaders in urban areas need to be extremely careful about the advice they give and the example they set. Church leaders who organize their congregations to pull together to help urban refugees are to be commended.

But before those pastors urge everyone in their congregations to stay in populated communities, they need to verify that at least 4,000 meals have been provided for every man, woman and child who stays. If the church intends to share food supplies with others in the community, then the church needs to be sure there are more than 4,000 meals per person. The church also needs to have plans and resources to cover the needs of the congregation once all the food supplies are exhausted. 4,000 meals will not last out the crisis, but they should last until a reasonable agricultural enterprise is underway.

Church leaders are right to see y2k as an opportunity for ministry. But too many church leaders seem to be looking at y2k as another ministry gimmick: three weeks of sloppy joe handouts in the parking lot, and then three weeks of follow-up after the grocery stores open again. Church leaders must not presume to think that the supermarkets will open within a three-year or a even a six-year period. They must realize that their congregations cannot take care of anyone in the community if they, too, are weakly scavenging for food. Pastors would also do well to realize that they do their congregations a grave disservice if they persuade them to stay in a high risk-area with inadequate resources for long-term survival.

Adequate organization of a church congregation must include the organization of the community into a coherent, productive agricultural region. Manpower and available land must be intelligently assigned to specific tasks. Someone, presumably the church leadership, needs to make the tough decisions about how much of produced food is stored, and how much is immediately given away. Above all, individual families must be coached on household preparation.

Some y2k books tell readers how to set up their single-family homes with bottled water reserves, wood stoves, stored food and chemical toilets. This advice presumes a very moderate y2k crisis that can be ridden out in any suburban home, rather like the riding out of heavy snowstorms or hurricane warnings: Lots of temporary inconvenience, but Blue Sky again soon.

I must be brutally clear in this book. Cities and suburbs could be literal ghost towns. Towns of 20,000 population could be spared the worst trials of urban chaos, but only if they currently meet certain criteria for neighborliness (extra warm), household guns-per-capita (high), and unemployment (almost non-existent). Urban survivalists who try to make a go of it in larger cities and suburbs will stand out if they appear to be making a go of it. The smoke coming out of that expensive

47

wood-burning stove could be the very thing sought by hungry gangs who will be looking for households that have prepared for and survived the first two weeks of y2k.

Evidence is mounting that electrical power will go out in every major metro area for "an extended period." No one knows if this period will last three months or three years. Even if it is only three weeks, the computers that control water supply and transportation will not be able to support anyone in those metro areas. In the process of leaving, hungry people would glean every crumb of food from every building. Some would pay for the crumbs, some would steal them.

This is why you must give careful thought to your location. If you stay in the city, can you survive the upheaval and the bleak aftermath? If you live within 200 miles of the big city, can you survive the waves of human refugees who pass you? If your goal is not survival, but to be in a place where you can help the needy, where can you accomplish the most good?

For the reasons listed in Appendix J, I think it would be great if families could team up with church leadership and work together to make their communities thriving, prosperous agricultural marvels. For some families who are not especially enterprising, I think just such an arrangement will be the best option for long-term survival -- to stay as close to an organized church as possible, contributing to a helpful effort. Ideally, it would be not just a church-wide effort but a community-wide effort. Thus, unprepared people in those communities could be wrapped safely into the arms of compassionate churches rather than being flung out of the community as starving refugees. But if the church leadership in those communities is weak, indecisive, and unwilling to mention the possible desolation of y2k, then individual families need to aggressively take their survival into their own hands. Remaining in any community with cowardly church leadership would be a mistake, because such a community is very likely headed for desolation.

If, therefore, you conclude that you must be a rural survivalist, the most important thing you can buy as you prepare for y2k is geographic safety -- in other words, a place in the country -- way out in the country. Your urban or suburban home will lose its value as a place to live and as an asset to sell. Y2k analysts believe urban real estate prices will crash by December, 1999 as residents drop everything and begin the migration out of the cities. Abandoned homes and apartments, if not harmed by scavengers, would deteriorate from lack of maintenance.

I happened to be in New Zealand in early 1998 during a freak power outage in the nation's largest city. Full power was not restored for several weeks. The situation has been studied by y2k analysts to see just what happens when power outages last more than ten minutes. Within two hours of the blackout the high rise apartments were being voluntarily evacuated because of sewage odor, and no one returned until power and water pressure were fully restored many weeks later. Residents said the smell was so unbearable that they couldn't go back to their apartments even for a moment to pick up a needed item. When electric water pressure pumps finally gained enough strength to pump water higher than the first floor, clean-up was an unpleasant and expensive task. In high rise office buildings, the situation was similar. In the early hours of the crisis, workers struggled to carry computers down dozens of flights of stairs in an effort to relocate business operations.

The survival suggestions in this book are not advice for temporary subsistence. The y2k crisis demands more. If you want to survive with a minimum of difficulties, you need to make a successful transition to a non-computer-dependent lifestyle in a safe geographic area. Don't follow a strategy of making contingency plans for possible inconvenience to your present lifestyle. If you have children, the most reasonable contingency to urban living in 2000 is urban evacuation. Pursue a strategy for starting a successful new lifestyle. Success in y2k survival doesn't mean knowing how to find emergency water in your toilet reservoirs or extra chemicals for your chemical toilet. It means having an unlimited supply of clean well water, a functioning septic system, and an ongoing supply of good food if the supermarkets are empty for more than four years. If you live in a city or a suburb, you need another place. You need a place where you can make it.

Because the move to alternate housing must happen before the chaos begins, a good number of urban families are planning to relocate to places outside the city before July, 1999. Some are planning to do it before July, 1998, so they have a little time to get things ready.

Some families will keep their city homes, but many are putting them up for sale, calculating that urban property values will be dropping as early as March 1999, and that their money will do more good in investments other than worthless, urban real estate. Not all are abandoning their city jobs, but many are, looking for more rural kinds of employment, and making drastic career changes based solely on their opinions about the severity of the y2k problem.

I mention this to emphasize the point that a lot of families are coming to the same unambiguous conclusions about the potential threat of y2k. Some are taking what others would consider the ultimate drastic step: totally relocating home, business and family, just because something serious might happen. *Forbes* magazine recently mentioned a y2k community called *Rivendell* in Virginia, where a number of families bought a large piece of agricultural land, divided it up and built homes on it. I just saw an ad in another national magazine for "America's best y2k community" somewhere near Pagosa Springs, Colorado.

I realize this kind of relocation is really a radical concept. Especially for wives who have put their hearts and souls into their homes. Even if we allow ourselves to think about the saddest dangers and hardships of y2k, nobody with roots in a nice community and memories in a nice home wants pull up and move. If your wife is one of those who want to stay put, please have her read the letter to Mrs. Smithwick in Appendix A.

Let me tell you how one family came to the decision to move. Let's call them the Joneses.

First, the Joneses acquainted themselves with facts. At first they threw the facts away because the facts were so uncomfortable. But then the Joneses started contemplating the consequences of those facts, and they had to admit this:

A whole series of irresponsible actions have put Americans in a precarious position that invites sudden social disorder. Personal debt is at an all time high, personal savings are at an all time low, exuberance about the stock market is irrational, and entire cities depend on computer technology that is not capable of functioning reliably in the year 2000. Not one bank, insurance company or government agency is ready for 2000. Some managers think they're ready for it just because they've hired a few programmers to take a look at their code. That's not "ready," because the code must be fixed, and it must be tested. Testing is the really hard part, because the results are variable and no test is 100% accurate. The best programmers are worried.

Every week they discover new surprises that complicate the rewriting process. Some of the better programmers who started "early" are discovering so many unforeseen complications that they are concluding that they must start the whole process over.

The Joneses found the best professional assessment of y2k they could, and then they thought about it. It went like this:

Every western nation waited too late to begin the repair. There is not an adequate standard that will allow repaired computers to talk to each other. It is doubtful that any system will be fully functional. A few small application programs may be running on the systems in time, but the embedded chip problem, the foreign problem (failure of other nations to be ready) or electrical power problem may ambush repaired computers anyway.

And so the Joneses concluded that America was looking at the high likelihood of social and economic disruption. Most disruptions cause ripple effects. History teaches that disruptions in the basics (food, water and fuel) really hurt big cities. History also teaches that rural, self-sufficient people fare best. These are some of the facts the Jones were trying to come to grips with.

They knew, of course, that simply moving out of a city into the country does not make one self-sufficient. Most country folks shop at the supermarket because it's easy. But if the supermarkets close, most country folks have land, tools, seeds and the know-how to keep food on the table.

In 1991, the Joneses were convinced they needed to get away from early 21st century turmoil which they thought would most likely be brought on by market implosions. This problem alone can cause many of the same hardships that a computer problem can cause -- the same dangerous ripple effects.

So the Joneses climbed into the car and went searching for a little homestead about 80 miles outside the big city...something with a little land for a garden, some room for small animals, and when they found a good spot, they bought it. They moved there in '92. Here are some of the lessons they learned that may help you in your decision.

They don't miss the city the way they thought they would.

They like the country, but it ain't easy being city-slickers on land that has never had a producing garden. It took them two years to prepare the ground, learn what to plant, how to harvest it, and how to store it.

This may make it sound like they became farmers. They didn't; they're still city-slickers who often commute to the city, shop at the supermarket, and stay involved in city affairs. They wouldn't even fit into the category of hobby farmers.

But they are trying to learn what it takes to grow edible food in case they might have to. They can do it on a very small scale, but it would be hard to grow enough to feed everyone in their family for a whole year. Or three years. But they could do it if they purchase some extra beans, wheat and rice and store it in their garage, which, incidentally, they have just done.

The Joneses took very drastic action. They left their comfortable city home and started living in an area in which there were strangers, and from which they were not able to earn as much income. They left the familiar for the unfamiliar.

Were they smart or foolish? If the y2k problem is remotely as bad as it might be, the Joneses might be one of the families who survive.

Should everyone in the city imitate the Joneses? Everyone in the city should understand that they might, in February, 2000, desperately wish they had kept up with these Joneses. We advise everyone in the cities to have, at the very least, an alternative place they can go outside the city if urban chaos disrupts city life. We understand that only a very small percentage will take our advice.

By all appearances, the Joneses are happy with their decision and their new lifestyle. Do they have any regrets about their decision to relocate? Only one: they're eighty miles outside the city, and just discovered that eighty miles may not be far enough because urban thieves and robbers aren't afraid to use brute strength to take food from those who have it. They start in their neighborhoods and keep moving out until their hunger is satisfied or until the crisis is over. The Joneses happen to be visible from the road, and this might invite an unwanted, well-armed truckload of intruders to stop in for an unfriendly visit.

So Mr. Jones is looking for another place that might be safer, a little farther out and a little better hidden. We asked Mr. Jones if he enjoys the process of moving. His comments are instructive.

"No. Hate moving. But, well, if the crisis lasts only three months, we'll be all right where we are. Believe me, I'm tempted to pretend and say, 'Aw...three months must certainly be all the longer it's gonna last.' But can I gamble my family's safety on what I wish would happen? If y2k lasts longer, my family will not be safe here, and I'm not going to bet my life, and their lives, on my wishful thinking."

Some people may think Jones is a paranoid extremist. The people who know him, however, know he's simply contemplating the possibility of ugly circumstances. Jones has let his mind grasp the potential, ugly aspects of a real emergency.

"Here's what I had to imagine," Jones explained. "I got out my calculator. If there's a power outage, people will flood out of the city. I figure that my county, which has about 10,000 people, will have about 330,000 by June of 2000. Each of my neighboring counties would have about that many too. If this y2k thing drags on because people panic, and if things like transportation take a long time to become functional again, our family will be living on the food stored in our cellar. We won't have a whole lot. My children could be hungry, and I don't mean ready for dinner. I mean they could be physiologically hungry. I don't want to have to make decisions about whether to shoot starving refugees, or let them steal my food and then watch my children starve.

"If we're in a more private location, that ugly deal may never come up. I don't want to shoot anybody. Plus, the more rural we are, the more food we might be able to grow, store and maybe share with people who wait too long to get out of the cities."

Now ask yourself this question: If grocery store shelves are bare, where would you want to be? In your apartment? Nervously standing guard over your last crust of bread?

Or would you rather be out in the countryside surrounded on all sides by productive farms and friendly farmers who know how to grow food and who may have tools and advice they're willing to share with their new city-slicker neighbor?

Please don't stop reading because this book has introduced an uncomfortable, bloody scenario. These are precisely the kinds of things you must think about in order to face the y2k problem. Y2k is not a plot from a movie, it's a real technological problem that will touch every person in America.

We can pretend otherwise if we want to, but our most noble wishful thinking will not change the effects of real, bone-crunching disaster that truly can be brought to millions of people by computer failure. Computers really do provide us our food, water, electricity, fuel, and paychecks.

If there is a shortage of these staples, violent thugs will take what they can, and they will be highly motivated to do so. Hunger is a strong motivater.

Most of the people I know who have relocated have taken seven simple steps to make themselves self-sufficient.

First, they have located and secured their rural house location.

For some families, it's not their primary residence. It's their escape place, and they go there on weekends to prepare garden plots, to add to compost piles, and to cut and stack firewood. Because late-model automobiles will have trouble operating in the year 2000, most of these folks plan to have moved there before November, 1999.

Their homes are not expensive second homes. Some are vacation cabins in the mountains. Some are trailers set at the far end of a farmer's land. Some farmers are willing to sell or rent an acre or so to industrious families who will live on the land and help the farmer keep a wary eye out for year 2000 thieves. Resourcefulness and creativity are two keys to surviving y2k problems, so don't be afraid to offer to buy something that may not formally be on the market.

Once a location is established, it is wise to drill a private water well, which is connected to either a hand pump or backup generator power. A **summary** of the advice offered by families who have successfully relocated goes like this:

- take care of your water situation first. Make sure you can get clean water without electricity. If the well is shallow, a freeze-proof hand pump and Katadyn water purifier bucket will give you what you need. Water purifiers are available from Ready Made Resources 800-627-3809.

-purchase a generator and enough stockpiled fuel to power

the generator for at least two years, and preferably three.
Available through China Diesel at 619-669-1995.

-connect at least one household circuit to the generator so a
refrigerator or battery chargers can be hooked up to power for
brief periods. If you can afford it, get a kerosene freezer.
Available from Lehman's at 330- 857-5757.

-purchase a wood stove that can serve as the primary heat
source in times of power outages (remember, pellet stoves require
electricity).

-acquire a large supply of firewood, and the tools needed to
get more.

-purchase a good deer rifle and a healthy amount of
ammunition. There will be a shortage of ammunition. One analyst
has predicted that when American dollars become worthless, single
rounds of ammo will be used as currency in some communities.

-prepare at least one acre of land for tilling.

-buy a selection of non-hybrid seeds. Sources listed in
Appendix G.

-acquire stored food staples of

Salt

Beans

Rice

Powdered Milk

Honey

Wheat grinder and wheat

Peanut Butter

Canned Goods

Vitamin C

Other Vitamins

Antibiotics

If you can do these things, you will be self-sufficient for as long as your supplies hold out. If you invest some time in learning how to hunt game, fish, and grow produce in good soil, you can replenish your supplies as you use them up and share them with others who were not as wise as you were.

I realize that many readers will react to this scenario as very strange, as something that would be more of a 19th century lifestyle. It is. If the y2k problems become as severe as some experts are predicting, every region of America, including suburbia, will be suddenly thrust back into 19th century conditions, and not just because many of the computers think it's 1900.

Is this an apocalyptic condition? Of course not. None of the people living and prospering in the 19th century thought they were living in apocalyptic conditions. Many of them were happy, content, and completely in control of their lives. They were not vulnerable to breakdowns in international technology, and they knew very well how to provide for family needs, year round.

Those of us who prepare for 19th century conditions will be in a comfortable position, and the crash of computer technology will not greatly disturb home or hearth.

CHAPTER 4
What Will Become of Your Civilization?

*"...Virtually everything from supply, generation, and distribution is
controlled by hardware and software...
there will be power disruptions if things are not fixed..."*

David Mann,
President of Nova Scotia Power

Electricity is the commodity that makes modern civilization
what it is. Without it, our cities are socially and economically
nothing. The greatest potential problem of the y2k problem is
electrical failure. Not just power outages, but power surges and
fluctuations caused by noncompliant computer software. For
some of these computers it might be better if they just quit
running. Unfortunately, some of them will go haywire instead.
Surges to some transformers could require repairs and
replacements that take months. Power outages to food storage
facilities and businesses even for two days could be dangerous to
entire cities.

The March 3, 1997 Business *Week* ran a story on the Year
2000 Problem. The article discussed the possibility that electrical
power generation may be at risk. What is significant is the quote
from an official with EPRI, the Electric Power Research Institute,

the U.S. power industry's "think tank." The expert says the industry doesn't know if power is at risk.

Over a year later, the power industry was not much farther along in their assessment of the problem. Kathleen Hirning of the Federal Energy Regulatory Commission says the industry still doesn't know if power is at risk.

These sources tell us two frightening things: One, there is ignorance about our vulnerability to lose power. Two, there is a lack of action to find out and correct the threat of breakdown.

"There will be facilities where they go in and turn on the machines and they won't go on," says Dean Kothmann, head of the technology division at engineering firm Black & Veatch, the world's largest provider of power plants.

According to Dr. Gary North, this is the greatest problem that has ever faced Western civilization, other than nuclear war. If the power grid goes down and stays down, Western civilization will go down and stay down. Yet the power company experts just don't know. They aren't sure. This civilization may be hanging on a thread, but the experts who are supposed to know don't know.

Dr. North researched the problem thoroughly, and then moved to a rural property with its own private natural gas well. He has installed three 10 kw natural gas generators in reserve.

Sherry Burns is the special agent assigned to research the millennium bug for the CIA. In a recent interview with Reuters News Service, she indicated that the failure of electrical power was at the top of her list of concerns. It's a huge security threat because it can bring down American civilization in ways that no weapons or act of terrorism ever could. It is her job to study the political, social and economic tumult of y2k and she knows that threat number one is the electrical power grid.

Electric utilities are only now becoming aware that

programmable controllers--which have replaced mechanical relays in virtually all electricity-generating plants and control rooms--may behave badly or even freeze up when 2000 arrives. Many utilities are just getting a handle on the problem. "It's probably six months too soon for anyone to try to guess the complete extent of the problem," says Charlie Siebenthal, manager of the Year 2000 program at the Electric Power Research Institute, the industry group that serves as an information clearinghouse. "We don't know" if electricity flow will be affected, he said.

Kathleen Hirning told a House Science Subcommittee in May, 1998 that electricity and fuel companies do not know the extent of their exposure to the millennium bug. She cautioned that without testing it is impossible to determine the impact of some embedded systems malfunctioning and the ensuing ripple effect across a portion of the grid.

At the latest in a series of House hearings on the outlook for computer failures in 2000, Hirning outlined the complex inter-connected system of the nation's power grid and its pipeline system for moving natural gas and oil. "Energy companies use computers to connect plants, refineries, district offices, and major administrative and operational systems that interface with large data centers," Hirning said.

"Computers are also used to remotely control transmission system breakers, coordinate power generation schedules, compensate for large transmission line breaks, and provide protection against voltage, current and frequency fluctuations," she said.

A millennium mistake could affect the microprocess and not only shut down the system at the site, but shut down all the systems connected to it at the time of the mistake.

On June 12, 1998 Sen. Christopher Dodd, a Connecticut

Democrat, said, ``Quite honestly, I think we're no longer at the point of asking whether or not there will be any power disruptions, but we are now forced to ask how severe the disruptions are going to be."

The scary thing about power plant failure is that so few power plant managers realize that their sites could shut down. Rick Cowles is a top level consultant to the power industry and he is frustrated that plant managers are not taking y2k seriously. He created a web site to increase awareness, and writes on the first page, "the premise of this website is exceedingly simple. In the days and weeks following January 1, 2000, the electrical supply infrastructure that we depend on to provide power to every home and business may no longer be able to do so. Indeed, it's possible that such service interruptions could occur even before the century change.

"Consider, for a moment, the implications of this premise. In our industrialized and techno-oriented society, the mere possibility of being without power for an extended period of time is clearly a scary thought. No lights. No heat. No running water. These are things residents of industrialized nations in the 20th and 21st centuries are ill-prepared to be without."

Expert Roleigh Martin explains why some systems will shut down: "Real-time systems can be very complex, and they are used to control or monitor very high-value processes. Typically, a power station will have scores of real-time systems. They have been bought for different reasons by different people over the years, usually mirroring the gradual development of the installation. The production processes are now dependent on the successful continuous operation of the real-time systems.

"Because the production processes are so valuable, production managers and engineering staff fear the failure of real-time systems. When real-time systems fail, high-value processes shut down, and the costs of unexpected shutdowns can be enormous. For a power station, the cost of an unexpected shutdown can be hundreds of thousands of dollars. The pressure to keep the production process running is great. As a result, production managers resist changes to embedded systems.

"This means that operating systems are not upgraded. Improved functionality is postponed. Hardware which is no longer supported by the manufacturer remains in use. The result is a bunch of aging systems, based on languages, packages **and processors** for which the skills are gradually being lost. Because of this culture, fixing the Year 2000 problems is more complicated than for banking or administrative applications. The systems are more difficult to audit, because some are so old that the information about them has been lost. Doing the triage is complicated, because there is a risk that taking the system through a mock millennium change will cause the process to fail, with huge cost penalties.

"So to fix the problems, we need people who understand embedded systems technology, the production processes, and the commercial impact of mistakes in a manufacturing environment. These people are rare."

Systems are not yet failing, because utilities are afraid to test or because they are putting it off. Because real-time systems tend to have a look-ahead of less than a month, the failures will come late in 1999.

In May, 1998, David Hall, an embedded-systems consultant at Cara Corporation, warned 80 congressional aides of certain-to-come power outages. "Every test I have seen done on an electrical power plant has caused it to shut down. Period. I know of no plant or facility investigated to this date that has passed without Y2K problems," he said. Added Hall: "Things like this come out and the mass media gets hold of it -- you're going to have shortages because of panic. How to communicate this to the public needs to be addressed."

Hall raises an interesting issue. Will there be a point at which the nation's denial turns to panic? Could it happen before 2000? Or will the public continue to chalk-up reports like this to unbelievable exaggeration? Will they convince themselves that it's hype from extremists?

Professionals like Hall and Cowles have been reporting this reality for a long time. The mainstream media knows this information and has printed some of it, but the public is still not ready to think about it. That's good news for the readers of this book. Once the public realizes the vulnerability of every family, there will be a run on the resources listed in the appendices of this book, and many families will have to do without the things they desperately need because there are not enough to go around.

Are you convinced that it's time for you to act? Please read on:

Nuclear power plants pose an especially worrisome problem. While their basic safety systems should continue to work, other important systems could malfunction because of the 2000 bug. In one Year 2000 test, notes Jared S. Wermiel, who is leading the millennium bug effort at the Nuclear Regulatory Commission, the security computer at a nuclear power plant failed by opening vital areas that are normally locked. For that reason, the Nuclear Regulatory Commission is in the process of issuing a letter requesting confirmation from utilities that their plants will operate safely come Jan. 1, 2000. Given the complexity and the need to test, "it wouldn't surprise me if certain plants find that they are not Year 2000-ready and have to shut down," says Wermiel.

Joel Skousen, a relocation consultant, tells his clients to stay far away from any Nuclear Power Plant and away from land downwind.

The greatest worry of electrical failure is the grid problem. America's electrical power grid is tightly interconnected. Even if the utility in your area finishes their work, other utilities could cause it to freeze-up because they are connected in a large interconnected grid arrangement. Small failures in one locality can be transferred in seconds across states to cause big failures in many cities simultaneously.

"The main concern is not with large utilities like Southern Co., but with smaller ones that are still on the grid," reports Jim Jones of the Atlanta-based Information Management Forum. "Smaller utilities could suffer outages that could cause a domino effect."

Southern Co., the Atlanta-based holding company of Georgia Power Co. and other Southeastern electric power utilities, has budgeted $85.6 million toward its Y2K efforts, with plans to spend $60 million in 1998.

What happens if smaller utilities decide they can't afford Y2k repair? What happens if a couple of small utilities go dark, taking down some of the bigger plants they are tied into? What if they do dark without hurting other power plants? Could they reboot their systems?

According to The American Geophysical Union's *Earth in Space* magazine of March 1997, this is the nightmare of the power industry.

"Once power is interrupted in large metropolitan areas, diversity of electric use on the network is lost. When power is restored, all thermostatically controlled electric loads come back on simultaneously. This stress, added to the higher demands of many devices such as motors and transformers, can draw up to 600% of normal load during restoration procedures.

" Such a blackout is also likely to cause transient voltage stresses and permanent damage to network equipment such as high-voltage breakers, transformers, and generation plants, which makes them unavailable for restoring power. Hours or days may pass before power can be restored. Oak Ridge National Laboratory assessed the potential impact of a widespread blackout in the northeastern United States from a geomagnetic storm event slightly more severe than the March 1989 blackout as a $3–6 billion loss in gross domestic product. This figure does not account for the potential disruption of critical services such as transportation, fire protection, and public security. Other assessments placed the 1989 and 1991 geomagnetic storm effects in a category equivalent to Hurricane Hugo and the San Francisco earthquake in their relative impact on the reliability of the electric power grid."

What this means is that the nightmare of nightmares is a rolling blackout that happens so fast utilities can't get off the grid fast enough to keep from being knocked out. If too many power plants go out at the same time, there may not be enough power anywhere else in the grid to get the dead plants jump-started again. America has never seen a really widespread, multi-region blackout. There has always been enough power somewhere to jump-start a dead system. In 2000, numerous systems could stay dark. One programmer wondered aloud if electrical power might be off for fifteen years, and then he added, "maybe for good."

According to Ross Anderson of Cambridge University's Computer Laboratory, especially worrying is the lack of preparation in countries who use the same kinds of technology for their power grids and telecommunications systems, but still see no problem with y2k.

In an interview with Reuters, Anderson pointed to the contrast between the policy of companies like British Telecommunications and countries like South Korea.

BT bought telephone hardware in the late 1980s and has spent around 500 million pounds making sure it is not destroyed by the millennium computer bomb. South Korea bought similar equipment at around the same time and has spent nothing, because they see no problem, says Anderson.

Anderson also said electricity generating plants are the linchpin of modern life. The millennium computer bomb places them in jeopardy. If power generation struck down economies like South Korea or Japan, vital components for western countries would soon dry up.

"Electric power is the critical utility. After more than about three days (of failure) everything just folds up. Trains, heat, refrigeration, water supplies all go. We'd be straight back to 18th and 19th century, and it would take 20 years to regain the lost economic capability," Anderson said.

If the rolling blackout threat wasn't bad enough, computer programming veteran Chuck Missler notes that, in addition, the earth is scheduled to have unusually heavy bombardments of solar flare radiation, which can also add unique stress to the power grid.

Missler relates a story to illustrate the fragility of the grid: In July 1996, way out in the middle of Nowhere, Idaho, electricity from a transmission line jumped to a cottonwood tree that had grown too tall next to that line. Zap. Instant short-circuit.

That outage, combined with the heat wave that was in progress at the time, caused a domino effect that cut power to 15

Western states and parts of Canada and Mexico.

Rides were shut down at the Fair in San Diego; subway cars in San Francisco's BART system stopped in their tracks; LA shut down seven of its giant water pumps...

Some banks, stores and restaurants had to close; others operated without cash registers, computers, lights and refrigeration. In northern Nevada, police in Reno and Sparks ran out of temporary traffic signals. In Boise, most offices and state agencies sent workers home and banks locked their doors during the outage.

This is an excellent example of what is known as the Y2K Domino Effect - one small problem causing dozens of big problems.

The domino effect is the problem of falling systems. One system fails, but another is dependent on it. Like a series of gigantic rows of dominoes, each within falling distance of another, so is the y2k problem and its effects. No one can even guess what these effects will be. This is what makes y2k the most complex problem facing the world -- possibly ever. Consider banking. Banks are threatened by y2k. Depositors will draw out cash. Then the system collapses. If a business cannot pay programmers because its bank is closed, it cannot complete its y2k repairs. When it fails, the firms it supplied are trapped by production shortages.

What happens to cities if gasoline is unavailable to truckers? If the computers that control train schedules break down? If rail freight cars cannot be located by defective computers? Think about your supermarket's shelves.

Here's another potential crisis: failures in farm production. Yes, farm activity way out in the country affects each one of us.

Modern commercial farming is tied to hybrid seeds.

CHAPTER 5
What Will Become of Your Money?

"The world of finance ... is especially vulnerable. ... (T)he absolute worst case ...is a global financial meltdown' ... Stocks held electronically ... could be wiped out. Interest might not be properly credited ... Deposits or trades might not be credited to an account.
... (T)he consequences may be catastrophic'"

Business Week, August 12, 1996

"(Alan Greenspan) pointed out that 99 percent readiness for the year 2000 will not be enough. It must be 100 percent. Thus, the message seems clear: all financial institutions must be ready; ...agencies....service providers....vendors...bank customers...and international counter parties must be ready."

Congressman James Leach,
November 4, 1997

The second greatest threat of the y2k crisis is bank failure. Students of the crisis predict that it will begin before the year 2000 as a financial calamity centered on banks' inability to stay open. In the unlikely event that electrical power stays up, banks will have a tough time staying open because of internal computer failure or because of computer interconnections with bank computers that infect and crash repaired computer systems.

73

To understand why a bank may have to close in 1999, consider the structure of American banking. Many Americans do not understand that bank vaults are almost empty. Banks earn their money by charging interest on loans. "Successful" banks loan out all the money they can, and they are usually the ones that attract the most business. The money they loan out is the money depositors have put in the bank. Sometimes depositors need to withdraw their money, and the banks operate on the hope that on the day that withdrawal is made, someone else is in the lobby making a deposit in the bank.

This is a dangerous way to run a local bank, and it's even more dangerous to run the federal banking system the same way. But that's how the big money center banks work, and how the Federal Reserve works. What if a financial crisis comes and more people want to withdraw their money than there are people who want to deposit money?

Well, the government wouldn't let that happen, right? Don't we have a government agency called the FDIC that insures all deposits up to $100,000? That's what the banks say, but FDIC funds can cover only a few small claims. In fact, the FDIC protects less than 1% of U.S. deposits. Let me repeat that. The FDIC protects less than 1% of U.S. deposits.

What percentage of depositors' funds are in the bank at any one time? With most banks, less than 20%. With some banks, there may be less than 5%.

During the y2k crisis, some banks may have to close because of public panic. Too many people may be coming in to withdraw cash. Other banks may have to close because of computer failures.

At a recent y2k conference for bankers, Brian Smith, Partner and Chairman of Year 2000 Task Force for Mayer, Brown

74

and Platt and Michael Ugliarolo, Managing Director of British Telecom Company presented some of the problems financial institutions will face. They pointed out that regulated institutions such as theirs would be the most severely impacted and also the most severely penalized if things go wrong.

The concept of "systemic risk" was put forward, meaning the potential threats to the linkages between systems that are necessary to do daily business. A non-compliant data transfer system could render an entire network unusable. This concern caused a cease-and-desist order against Putnam-Green Financial Corp. for year 2000 violations. The FDIC and the Georgia Department of Banking demanded the same from Putnam-Green's three subsidiaries. They were charged with operating inadequate and unreliable electronic information systems and failing to ensure those systems could perform data processing after December 31, 1999. Putnam-Green needs to have all their systems tested by December 31 of this year and be using only fully compliant systems in their actual operations by no later than July, 1999.

It was pointed out that once the issues and the possible ramifications of y2k are understood by the lender, it becomes just another factor of business risk to assess and determine loan eligibility and shouldn't be more difficult to handle than any other business factor.

Banks also need to review their current portfolios for potential y2k risk. Y2k risk factors can be worked into existing credit standards and applied to any customer. The presenters emphasized that concentrations of credit need to be looked at carefully. It might be that some banks have targeted certain industries that are potentially sensitive to y2k. Manufacturers with significant embedded logic in their production facilities such as refineries or chemical plants are examples. Any large customer needs to be scrutinized for possible loan problems. Business plans and y2k planning need to be looked at quarterly from now on. If y2k hardware problems cause these manufacturers to close, their banks will close.

These closings could produce a ripple effect not unlike the same effect seen in the first Great American Depression. It was horrible, and it caught almost everybody by surprise. It happened during days of exuberant stock market speculation when attitudes about a soaring market and the great "roaring twenties" were identical to today's optimism about indestructible mutual funds.

The Great Depression was triggered by a massive stock market crash in 1929. In a few weeks investors lost a sum almost as great as America's total cost in fighting World War I. Money was short everywhere. Employers simply could not stay afloat. In Donora, Pennsylvania, for example, only 277 people out of 14,000 were left with a job. When employers pink-slipped workers, those workers pulled savings out of their banks to pay their bills. So many people were pulling their money out that other depositors worried that the banks would run dry. They too lined up at the teller's window, and by 1933 over 10,000 banks had closed in order to keep from losing every dollar to panic-stricken depositors. On March 3 of 1933 President Roosevelt closed all remaining 18,000 banks.

The first folks to make the withdrawals were the lucky ones. Other depositors lost their life savings because they did not act ahead of the ripple effect. They lost out because the banks didn't have enough money for everyone.

The same ripple effect could sweep through America again without a stock market crash, and here's how:

Think about it as a domino effect. Imagine that America's businesses, including the one that employs you, are the dominoes.

Computer failures will be the trigger effect that starts the dominoes falling. An office of the Federal Reserve reported in 1997 that only 11% of banks were working to fix their computers. The Senate Banking Committee fears that few banks will be ready for the year 2000. If even a few computer failures force just a few banks to close, American middle-class depositors will begin to fear for their deposits - their checking accounts, their CDs, their savings accounts, their IRAs...

...and the first families to drive down to the bank for a withdrawal will be the lucky ones, because by the next day the banks will start running low on available cash to give those depositors, and will have to start closing their doors to protect what's left.

Today there are many living Americans who remember the dark days of the Great Depression, and who remember that banking was what kept American business humming. These folks will probably be the first in line to recover their money, because they know how the ripple effect works: if banks close, the truck driver can't be paid because the grocer who needs that trucker can't write him a check for the delivery. The grocer can't pay him with cash, because he doesn't have any cash, because shoppers didn't have any to spend because they couldn't get any out of the bank. And besides, why would shoppers want to shop at a supermarket with empty shelves because the trucks didn't arrive? Crash go the dominoes.

What about credit cards? Credit card machines are already rejecting cards with "00" expiration dates. Lawsuits on this issue are already starting to fly. If banks begin closing in '99, credit card companies would have to invalidate all cards because banks would not be able to pay the balances. Paychecks also could become worthless because there would be no bank open to cash

or deposit them. Businesses could not issue or pay invoices for the same reason, and businesses could begin to close as fast as dominoes can fall. When unemployment reaches a certain level, no one buys any goods or services anyway, and that only accelerates the fall of the dominoes.

Our society depends on banking transactions, and that's why bank closings can create serious depressions that ultimately even depress governments because they can't stay solvent when their tax collectors can't cash tax payments and they can't pay their employees, can't issue social security payments, and can't help the poor.

Yes, even wealthy governments can find themselves as broke as everyone else. But the interesting thing is this: Even in the great depression, life went on, trade went on, and some average people became very wealthy. Even without U.S. dollars. Some communities printed up their own currencies. One drug store issued special sea shells as currency.

But all through history, the medium that holds its value and serves as a basis for consistent trade and wealth-building is gold.

People who have enough spendable gold should be able to survive y2k and maintain their financial dignity. Let me pause right here and say that this book is not a "get-rich-off-the-y2k-problem" book. It's a preserve-your-family book. The following recommendations should help you hold on to your financial dignity.

What is financial dignity? It is the state of *honest, orderly solvency*...which is nothing more than a fancy phrase for *financial freedom*. People with financial dignity have enough money for what they need. It's their money. It doesn't belong to others. They have control over their wealth, even if the banks close or the government outlaws greenbacks. But most importantly, they have

control over their lives.

The biggest enemy of financial dignity is personal debt. For the reasons described earlier, you need to sell anything you can that will become worthless in 2000, including your urban or suburban real estate. If you can get rid of all your debt before 2000, it could be a very responsible thing to do. Try not to go into debt when you get your country place. If a bank holds your mortgage, and they need money to pay all those depositors standing at their windows, they will repossess your home real fast if you miss a payment. They will sell your house for whatever they can get and give the cash to depositors just to stay open. In the first Great Depression, thousands of families were forced out onto the streets, their only homes the shanties they could build of scrap lumber.

Banks will also be selling repossessed cars, land, tools, businesses...

And the people who will be buying these for pennies on the dollar are the people who have cash.

Until you are out of debt, you are a true slave of various lenders and employers. Your future does not belong to you, but to a bank, a union, the IRS or the county court. Y2k will not change that fact, it will make it worse.

Even if the banks close, they have records of your debt and will come after it as they can. It is when the banks close that the situation gets dangerous. To satisfy FDIC claims, the Fed will have to print money out of thin air. When they start doing this, the value of each dollar will fall. As the dollar falls, the value of gold will go higher and higher. If you own gold in a form that won't be confiscated by the government, your purchases will go even farther.

If, in January 2000, there is no electricity to run the

government printing presses, then the value of the dollar can fall only so far. But if the electricity is off, so is business, and the case for gold becomes stronger.

Some people ask, "if gold will be so valuable, why don't I mortgage my house again, take the cash and buy gold? When it appreciates, I can pay off the house with gold and still have some left over!"

I know one man who is following this strategy, but he fully understands that he may lose his house, and that he can't predict how far or how fast gold will rise. He happens to be in a position in which he can afford to lose his home to the bank. You might justify gambling with your urban property, but do not gamble with your country retreat.

Is it ethical to borrow from a bank to finance some of your y2k preparation? Yes, as long as you believe you will be able at some point to pay that bank back. And as long as you can get along without the collateral, if the bank takes it.

This book is not giving and cannot give financial advice, but it should be pointed out that the y2k experts most respected by the editor have all purchased gold, and that all of them expect it to appreciate from its present low levels.

Some people ask, "Isn't it risky to own gold because the government could confiscate it?"

The U.S. government still does have the authority to confiscate gold. It has done so four times. But it has never confiscated gold coins that have value to collectors. It is these coins that will probably be the more ready, most valued form of currency between the years 2000-2010.

Gold is remarkably stable and reliable. With the exception of two years (1974 and 1980) gold has had little or no price volatility for hundreds of years.

When the Asian currencies recently lost half their value, Asians who owned gold lost nothing. Author James Cook recounts that the Empires of Byzantium and Rome both began their declines when they trifled with the value and importance of their gold standard and gold coinage.

You can buy gold coins from local coin dealers, but before you do, check prices by calling ICA (800-525-9556) or IRI (800-328-1860 [ask for Kal Gronvall]), or Franklin Sanders (901-853-6136), three reputable national dealers.

So what will become of your money that's not converted into gold, tools, food, or other valuable, appreciating property? If it's still in the banks, it could be lost for good. Sen. Christopher Dodd, D-Conn., said there likely will be "a deluge of litigation" against banks and financial companies by consumers who lose money.

That warning came during Senate hearings held at the time the White House released a report concluding the federal government is moving too slowly to fix the millennium problem. Of the nearly 4,500 critical computer systems the government must repair, including those for national defense, air traffic control and income taxes, only 6% are claimed to have been fixed, according to the report by the Office of Management and Budget.

The financial industry, too, is running out of time to repair the problem, experts told the Senate panel. Companies need to have a solution in place by the end of 1998 in order to allow a year for testing in 1999, said Larry Martin, president of Data Dimensions Inc., a consulting firm based in Bellevue, Wash.

"The ability of international banks to operate effectively after the year 2000 is, in our estimate, seriously in question," said Martin.

If there are bank failures resulting from the year 2000 problem, taxpayers would ultimately foot the bill for any government bailout, noted Jeff Jinnett, president of LeBoeuf Computing Technologies. But this observation, and those about litigation, presuppose that the government, including its tax collecting and court systems are working. Even if electricity and government offices continue to run, the outlook for the economy is not good.

One large U.S. bank, BankBoston NA, expects to spend some $50 million over four years to cope with its 2000 problems, said David Iacino, senior manager of the bank's Millennium Project. Even if a bank is prepared, it could be adversely affected by its close links to other financial institutions that are not, Iacino said.

The parent of the Nasdaq Stock Market, the nation's second-largest, started its y2k repair program in June 1996 at a cost of around $20 million, Nasdaq President Alfred R. Berkeley III told the subcommittee. How many banks can afford this? How many businesses can afford a y2k repair project?

Early reports of the sheer expense of y2k repair looks like this:

City of Corpus Christi: $10 million, Source: Corpus Christi Caller Times. Aetna: $95 million, Business Today. State of Maine: $12 million, Business Today. U.S. Government: $4.7 billion, Government Computer News/OMB. BankBoston: $75 million, Business Today. Citicorp: $600 million, Reuters. Filenes Basement, $6.9 million, Boston Globe. Union Carbide $50 million, Reuters. Continental Airlines, $12 million, Reuters. Chase Manhattan Corp., $300 million, American Banker. Fleet Financial Group, less than $150 million, American Banker. NationsBank, $120 million, American Banker. J.P. Morgan & Co., $250 million,

American Banker. BankAmerica Corp., $380 million, American Banker. General Motors, $500 Million, Wall Street Journal. Columbia/HCA Healthcare, $60 million, Atlanta Business Chronicle. Amoco Corp., more than $100 million, Atlanta Business Chronicle. Atlanta's Life of Georgia, $3.5 million, Atlanta Business Chronicle. Credit Suisse Group, $330 million, Istituto Bancario San Paolo di Torino, $56 million, Reuters. Houston Industries, $155 million, Dow Jones News Service.

This is only a partial list, but the $7.96 billion dollar total gives an idea of how the economy can be impacted. The Gartner Group estimates total repair costs to be $650 Billion. Even if there was not a potential technological shut-down, the economic strain on the corporate bottom-line could set the American economy reeling. Y2k expenses are simply stay-in-business expenses. They don't build the business. They hurt stockholders' bottom line.

Thus y2k hammers American business from several directions. Business *Week Magazine* reported at the end of 1997 that the y2k bill can be astronomical. In 1997 alone, CSX Corp. spent $35 million to $40 million on Y2K, says Chief Information Officer John Andrews, and the company is only 30% finished with the process.

If some smaller businesses choose to close rather than bear the expense of fixing their code, what will that mean to the larger companies they used to supply? Small companies that quit, or fail to get ready, can literally cause larger companies to go out of business. General Motors is extremely concerned that small suppliers could force them out of business. GM has 85,000 suppliers, very few of whom understand what they must do to prepare their own software. It is estimated that more than half have not even begun to assess their y2k vulnerability. Remember what happened to GM when just two brake suppliers went on strike for 17 days. It closed 26 of 29 GM plants and cost them $900 million dollars. In the same way, it may be the small companies that ruin the big ones in the year 2000 - even the big ones who spend hundreds of millions to prepare their own systems to work. The same is true with banks. The small ones could ruin the large ones. Indeed, the larger banks are building teams of attorneys who are standing ready to sue the smaller banks, but it won't be lawsuits that save the US from the Millennium Bug. Those lawsuits, which are expected to top $1.3 *trillion* in settlements, will only serve to create a new specialty for attorneys. That is, if the electricity is on. As economist Ed Yardeni points out, if the power goes off, we won't even know if we have a y2k problem.

Y2K could also wreak havoc on governments, says *Business Week*. According to a U.S. Office of Management & Budget report issued on Dec. 16, barely one-quarter of federal systems are ready for Year 2000. One big trouble spot: the Transportation Dept., which operates the air traffic control system. Overall, Washington will spend nearly $4 billion fixing Y2K in more than 8,500 separate systems.

Even if nearly all the nation's banks and financial institutions become prepared for 2000, a highly publicized computer system failure of one of them could have a negative impact on stocks of other financial companies, some experts believe.

Computer experts have an even bigger fear. The failure of that one figurative institution could bring the others down in another way -- by contaminating good data with the failing company's bad data.

If any two institutions trade data, corrupted data in one

system could corrupt entire other systems. What does it take for one computer's data to be corrupted? One uncorrected line of code that causes havoc with the overall system. Thus one measly line that's missed by the reprogrammers (out the several billion that need checking) could easily bring down dozens of banks or other institutions.

This is why Alan Greenspan has said that 99% y2k readiness is not enough for the banking industry. It must be 100%.

What's really significant about the legacy banking systems is that the banks have had 30-40 years to shake almost all of the defects out of their computer systems. Even today, under normal circumstances, there will be the occasional hiccup; interest payments will sometimes be incorrect, deposits or withdrawals will be double-booked, etc.

Programmer Ed Yourdon points out that the real problem with the y2k projects in the nation's banks (and, in a similar vein, the other banks around the world) is that all of the software will be investigated, corrected to eliminate y2k problems, and tested as thoroughly as possible until time runs out on New Year's Eve, 1999 – but there will still be residual errors that will gradually become evident during the first few years of the new decade. A bank whose portfolio of computer applications contains 100 million program instructions, and whose programmers are geniuses on a par with the very best in the world may wrap up their work at the very end of the decade with only a hundred residual bugs; the typical bank will have 10,000 such bugs; and the worst will have as many as a million defects. According to some programmers, even one defect could crash the bank's system or infect another bank's system.

In summary, it looks like your dollars are doomed. Even in the best case scenario, your business could close or your present level of income be severely cut back. Your savings could vanish if your bank closes before you withdraw those dollars to a position of safety.

So when should you politely and quietly withdraw your funds from the bank? There will probably be no panic before April 30, 1999, but there is no guarantee of public self-assurance. The point of this chapter is to help you see that the value of paychecks and savings accounts will disappear, but that the value of a country place, stored food and supplies could be priceless. After April, 1999, every day your assets are in a bank will be a day those assets are at high risk of permanent loss. Every day and dollar invested in strengthening your country position is a vast increase in the value of your estate.

In a recent test of 2,500 PCs, 82 per cent failed to roll over to the year 2000 properly, and of those that failed nearly a quarter did so because of the RTC, even though the BIOS was working properly.

The bottom line is that if you have a PC or laptop on your desk, there is a 70 to 80 per cent chance that it will not be fully y2k compliant. To test your computer, check with the manufacturer before you do anything. Some tests are fine for some models, but could possibly damage other models.

Even if you don't own a "personal computer," you probably own three or four hundred microprocessors - sophisticated computers scattered throughout your home and your car - and you are more dependent on this computer hardware than most people are on their desktop computers.

This hardware is known as "the embedded chip." It has been estimated that there are 35 to 40 billion tiny microprocessors in appliances, cars, elevators, office security systems, medical equipment, satellites, power plants, sewer valves, oil pipeline valves, assembly line robots, nuclear power temperature sensors, and other things we depend on. A few are clearly faulty. But for others, not even engineers with detailed schematics can guarantee faultless performance in 2000. We can't really know if those little chips will fail or not until The Day. Paul French, an official in the Iowa State Department of Transportation, said this in an interview with Paul Dorr, a y2k consultant: "Quite honestly, GM's top people have said that cars won't start, come Y2k."

This is because of the embedded chip or the "embedded systems" in the cars. The US computer industry has forecast a failure rate of 500 million, or 2 per cent of the 25 billion chips installed in electronic components worldwide, but cannot identify which 2 per cent. . . .

The Computer Information Center reports that it is unlikely that the supplier of products containing the embedded processors would be able to tell you within a reasonable time (24 hours) where these processors are, what they do, or how they are affected by the Year 2000 Date Problem.

The center released a list of operations that contain chips whose failure would cause damage.

Accounting

Contact Managers/Organizers

Contracts

Credit control

Databases

Decision Support

Desk-top/Notebook/PDA Applications

Direct Mail

Distribution

HelpDesk

Legal

Maintenance

Manufacturing

Marketing

Membership/Loyalty Schemes

Operational

Order processing

Payroll

Personnel

Point of sale

Purchase ordering

R & D

Retail

Sales

Security
Spreadsheets
Stock control
Transport
Warehousing

Embedded Processes and Process Control Systems
Here is a list of some of the systems that might have embedded micro-controllers.

Office systems and mobile equipment
Answering machines
Copiers
Desktop computers
Faxes
Laptops and notebooks
Mobile Telephones
PDAs, Personal organizers
Still and video cameras
Telephone systems
Time recording systems
Voice mail
Building systems
Air conditioning
Backup lighting and generators
Building management systems
Burglar and Fire Alarms
CCTV systems
Door locks
Fire Control systems
Heating and ventilating systems
Lifts, elevators, escalators

Lighting systems
Safes and vaults
Security access control systems
Security systems
Security cameras
Sprinkler systems
Switching systems
Manufacturing and Process Control
Automated factories
Bottling plants
CAD systems
Energy control systems
Manufacturing plants
Nuclear power stations
Oil refineries and related storage facilities
Power grid systems
Power stations
Robots
Switching systems
Water and sewage systems
Time/clock stamps
Transport
Airplanes - air control, avionics, cabin systems,
electrical, flight systems,
mechanical/hydraulic and propulsion.
Trains
Buses
Marine craft
Jetties
Automobiles
Air Traffic Control Systems

92

Signaling Systems
Radar Systems
Traffic Lights
Ticketing systems/machines
Car parking and other meters
Transport passenger information systems
Check-in
Baggage handling
Emergency equipment
Command and control systems
Speed cameras, Radar speed detectors
Photo surveillance systems

Telephone exchanges
Cable systems
Telephone switches
Satellites
Global Positioning System (GPS) problem
Nuclear Industry
Security computers
Plant process (data scan, log, and alarm)/
Safety parameter display system computers
Emergency response systems
Radiation monitoring systems
Dosimeters/readers
Plant simulators
Engineering programs
Communication systems
Inventory control system
Technical specification surveillance tracking
Banking and finance

Automated teller systems
Credit card systems
Medical
Imaging equipment
Domestic equipment
Catering equipment
Central Heating control
VCRs

Credit cards
Licenses

In November, 1997, the US Congress heard testimony from an expert witness from the Gartner group about embedded chips. Here is what Congress was told:

"Most of the computers in the world are not performing desktop functions. For example, in 1995, Dataquest estimated that more than 3.3 billion microcontroller chips were shipped; these are computers with word lengths from four to 32 bits embedded in hardware such as cars, video recorders, elevators, microwave ovens, access control systems, navigation equipment (e.g., GPS), nuclear power plants and weapons. Many such systems are date-aware. In some cases, failure might cause serious business consequences, so the systems must be investigated as part of a year 2000 project.

"Many organizations in sectors such as manufacturing and utilities own non-desktop systems used for process control, monitoring and factory automation.

"International commerce can be affected by the failure of air traffic control systems anywhere in the world. The same can be said for interruptions due to failure in postal and package delivery

systems. International trade agreements will mean nothing if the mechanisms for trade -- communications, finance, production, and logistics break down between countries. Year 2000 focus must be contained in all current and future trade agreements.

"Both embedded and non-desktop systems pose particular challenges and are likely to be more difficult to identify, test and correct than "normal" computer applications. . . .

"Unlike "normal" computer software, failure of embedded systems frequently cannot be mitigated by manual systems. The national security can be impacted by the failure of weapon systems that could leave the country and/or its allies vulnerable - at best. Action must be taken to assure compliance of all of these systems is a high priority. Power suppliers, frequently linked in a "Grid", must assure uninterrupted power, or whole regions could shut down. Failure of communication systems could shut down international commerce."

Remember the economist, Dr. North, who moved to a remote place where he can generate his own electricity from natural gas generators? He discovered that electrical power is threatened by the chips in the power plants. He writes, "Up to 5% of embedded systems are not 2000-compliant. There is no easy way to identify which 5% these are. Systems managers must now identify the bad ones one by one, replace them one by one (including upgraded ones that, sadly, do not exist), and test the upgraded system. That is to say, this will not be done. We will go into 2000 not knowing.

"We are literally headed into what could be the collapse of this civilization -- if the power grid goes down, count on it -- without being able to verify the extent of the risk of systemic failure. We are being asked to sit tight: 'Wait and see.' But the stakes are total."

Dr. North then cites a story from *Electronic Engineering Times* (December 8, 1997) in which Ron Wilson suggests a scenario that illustrates the scope of the embedded chip problem:

> PRUDHOE BAY, ALASKA. - It is January 1, 2000. Far to the south in the Lower 48, information systems managers are shaking off the effects of the New Year's Eve party of the century, and checking in to verify that their data-processing systems survived the change of calendar. But here on the North Slope, there is a somewhat more pressing problem. Somewhere down the pipeline, a pumping station has shut down and refuses to answer. Minute by minute, a cylinder of crude oil reaching halfway across the tundra is getting colder, turning to sludge. Once frozen, it will not thaw until spring.

Potential tragedies like this one are possible because there are so few tools available to test and then fix the chips that lie hidden in remote pieces of equipment. Oil pipelines, satellite circuits, undersea oil rig valves, sewage backwash valves, and even the water supply circuits that prevent sewage and fertilizers and other harmful chemicals from flowing backward into the clean water supply.

"The bottom line is, we simply don't know how many embedded control systems will be affected," said Ray Alderman of the Embedded Software Association.

"Estimates by industry analysts suggest that the number is not large. Perhaps 5 percent of embedded systems will misbehave when their real-time clock ticks zero, less than two years from now. But a wide range of organizations, from automated manufacturing lines to public utilities to the operators of the Alaska pipeline, are chilled by one thought: They don't know which 5 percent. . . ."

From a Report on EPRI Year 2000 Embedded Systems Workshop, we learn that during a routine shutdown of a 500 MW power plant in England, a date roll-over test was conducted on the control system. Twenty seconds after the date was changed, the plant shut down. The shutdown cause was traced to a "smart" flue stack temperature sensor. The sensor was programmed to integrate and average temperature over a specific time period to minimize fluctuation of the output temperature. The program in the firmware on the chip utilized a real-time clock that depended on the actual date to calculate the time differential. The report concluded that there are no programming standards in place that dictate how a programmer obtains time intervals. The result is a great deal of uncertainty as to how each program is written and how time related calculations have been implemented.

Brian Watts, Chairman of the Australian Computer Society, noted that a US sewage treatment plant found that a couple of hundred of its valve control systems were going to release untreated sewage into a river in the year 2000.

Phillips Petroleum Co. engineers ran Year 2000 tests on an oil-and-gas production platform in the North Sea. The result: In a simulation, an essential safety system for detecting harmful gases such as hydrogen sulfide got confused and shut down. In real life, that would have rendered the platform unusable. Similar problems can occur in almost any sort of modern manufacturing that involves sensors and "smart" machinery.

Journalist Julia Vowler reported on a sample embedded chip problem, pointing out that testing one particular machine doesn't mean that identical models will test the same way.

"Pharmaceutical company Smith Kline Beecham has found that out. It bought two machines for monitoring and recording the performance of drug production. When they tested one, it

handled January 2000 very well, and they were very happy. But when they tested the other - same machine, identical chips - it didn't."

The scary explanation for the anomaly, when the firm checked serial numbers with the manufacturer, was that the chips had come from different makers, one of whom had made them year 2000 compliant, while the other hadn't. Documentation down to this level of detail is often not specified in the world of embedded systems. And these were machines that had been made last year."

Utilities consultant Roleigh Martin passed on a report from an observer who wished to remain nameless. In the testing of two coal-fire power plants in his city (which were currently off-line and being used as "hot spares") for year 2000 compliance, the clocks were simultaneously rolled over to the year 2000, causing immediate plant failure. In an attempt to better understand the failure, the roll over test was repeated. In the second test, the plants again failed, but a different embedded controller was determined to be at fault.

The roll-over test was repeated a third time in hopes of replicating one of the previous failures. In this test, the plants failed from yet a different embedded controller. It was determined that this last failure would have caused a portion of the grid to fail had the plants been on-line. It took 13 days in order to restore the plants to working condition from the last failure.

This kind of variable test result is what is so aggravating about y2k repair. The millennium bug is sneaky. It's full of surprises. Programmers used to think fixing a simple two-digit problem would be easy. It is rather simple, but because complex computer code is so interconnected and interdependent on other

complex functions of software as well as hardware, proper repair and testing may take up to ten times longer to test, fix, retest, fix and retest until everything works. Until the tests are conclusive of complete success, there are new disappointing surprises with y2k repair every day.

Author Victor Porlier cites the experience of CalTrans. Even though microchips in building operations and standard office equipment have many features in common, most embedded systems are unique to each enterprise. In the testing of the chips in their operations, CalTrans has found that two percent are going to be a problem. "That means that if there are 25 billion chips worldwide, we have to find the [500] million with date-aware, date-required, date-processing functions that Y2K will trigger."

"The problem is compounded," said the CalTrans spokesman, " because you can't duplicate the embedded system environment for testing like you can a software application; for many devices you can't roll the date forward without destroying the equipment." CalTrans has found that those buildings put up or remodeled between 1985 and 1993 are particularly vulnerable to Y2K embedded systems problems.

Two years ago Bill Gates claimed that both Windows 95 and NT were y2k compliant. He was surprised to find out recently that they are not. One of America's biggest planning and resource companies was recently asked to check the code of several large corporations - code that was believed to be completely repaired and ready for January 1, 2000. Code from seven major corporations was examined. It was discovered that there were numerous errors in each corporation's "fix" that would completely shut down that corporation's operations.

A recent and dramatic Y2k embedded system example was brought to the attention of the readers of the St. Louis Post

Dispatch on November 19, 1997 in a column by Virginia Hick. The article writes of an interview with Peter de Jager who was speaking locally on Y2k issues. Hick writes: "De Jager talked recently with an executive of a company that makes a volatile gas -- he would not identify the company more specifically -- who told de Jager how his plant discovered the seriousness of faulty embedded chips. The plant found a chip that failed when the date was moved forward. When the chip failed, it shut off a valve that would have shut down the cooling system. A cooling system shutdown, the executive said, would have caused an explosion. 'That was great news,' de Jager said. 'Because they checked - there will be no explosion. They're replacing the chips.' De Jager worries about the companies that are not checking."

In the same way PC microprocessors will surprise people who were told their PCs were year 2000 compliant, many of these chips will surprise us, too. Many are hard to test. Many are impossible to replace, especially those whose manufacturers went out of business years ago . Many are too expensive to replace. And many will be overlooked or forgotten until their failure reminds us where they are and what they do. In many systems, like your automobile electrical system, one chip failure can shut down the entire system. Sometimes, everything just stops. Other times, things go haywire and people get hurt. According to computer experts, one faulty chip was to blame for the chemical leak in the industrial disaster that killed 7,000 and injured 300,000 in Bhopal, India in 1984. The plant is reported to have had some 17,000 chips that worked fine, but the malfunction of just one was the culprit that sent a deadly chemical cloud over the city.

This is why some experts believe the "embedded chip" problem will be the most harmful y2k ambush of all. Comments

author Peter DeJager, "People are going to die, and that's what it's going to take to get some people to wake up to the y2k threat."

The Institute of Electrical Engineers of England says that the industry manufactured 7 billion embedded chips in 1996, that an unknown percent of them are doing date-sensitive tasks, (they are estimating 5-15%), but no one knows for sure where they are, so you have to inventory and test every chip. As noted earlier, some chips cannot be located, and others simply cannot be accurately tested.

Some companies who know the inventory task is risky at best are playing it safe. They are releasing only chip-free products. No microprocessors of any kind are installed. Maytag is now selling new washing machines that look slick and modern on the outside, but have 1950s components inside. The actual hardware is not old, but rather built on the perfectly good 1950s designs.

About the only way to adequately guard against the embedded chip ambush is to be in a safe, chip-free environment in January 2000. Some y2k specialists have said publicly that this is their intention, and that they will not be in or near airports, automobiles, hospitals, factories or workplaces on the enigmatic day, or on several days before and after that day.

If the chip problem is so bad, why hasn't the media been reporting on the problem? Certainly, they could say more, but they have been talking about chip failure. From May, 1997 to May 1998, Dr. North located over 85 related media stories. You can read these by accessing http://www.garynorth.com/y2k/results_.cfm/Noncompliant_Chips.

The headline subjects of these stories tell a story in themselves:

Embedded Systems: Chips with Y2K Failure Built In;

Noncompliant Chips in British Hospitals: Manslaughter!;

Dead Engines in Fire Trucks;

How Widespread Is This Problem? Very.;

How Important Is This Problem? Very.;

BAT Industries Sounds the Alarm;

Pharmaceutical Industry at Risk;

Chips Older Than 3 Years Are Almost Impossible to Replace;

50 Million Devices Will Produce Anomalies;

Vulnerable Systems: PBX Telecommunications;

Medical Equipment Could Shut Down, Permanently;

How Electrical Systems Can Go Haywire;

National Science Foundation Sounds a Warning;

This Problem Is Being Ignored;

Oil Industry Begins to Wake Up Late;

Worse Than the Mainframe Problem, Says Specialist;

A Catastrophe Looms, Says Y2K Expert;

Crucial Systems Are Hard to Repair;

This Is the Biggest Unknown of Y2K, Says Specialist;

The "Guardians of Our Lives" May Fail;

The Extreme Vulnerability of Hospitals;

Nuclear Regulatory Commission Warns FDA;

Summary Letter on the Embedded Chip Problem;

One-Fifth of Britain's Systems May Go Down;

It's Worse: Beyond Previous Estimates;

Testing Chips May Be More Work Than Locating Bad Ones;

FDA Warns Medical Device Manufacturers, Sort of;

Knoxville, Tennessee, Faces Embedded Chips Problem;

Questions for Utility Company Engineers: Embedded Chips;

Britain Lacks Engineers Familiar With the Problem;

What Could Go Wrong? Just About Everything;

Warning from the State of Idaho;

The Threat to the Power Industry;

Oil Drilling Rigs: Filled With Embedded Chips;

Rate for Significant Problems: 5% to 50% ;

A Very High-Risk Situation: Kappelman;

If These Systems Are at Risk, Everything Is at Risk;

Health Care Industry's Vulnerability;

Health Care: Lives at Stake;

The Threat Is Total, Gartner Group Tells Congress;

Leap Year Malfunction:One Company's $1Million Loss;

Defective Pacemakers = Patients at Risk = Lawsuits;

Widespread Problem, Says Joint Announcement;

50 Million Points of Darkness;

Manufacturers Are Flying Blind into a Disaster;

Minnesota Lists Problem Areas for Repairing Systems;

Diesel Locomotives and Cars: Forced Maintenance Chips;

A Corporate Disaster Recovery Plan Is Vital;

Warning from Expert: Huge Risk to the Public;

Programmer Warns of Disaster, Calls on Others to Get This Fixed;

Warning from a Power Company's Y2K Project Manager;

Early Test: Down Goes the Building's Automatic Lighting System;

Electrical Utility in England Admits the Problem;

Alaska Pipeline: A Gigantic Frozen Candlestick?;

Examples of Vulnerable Systems: Steel Plant, Pipeline, Refinery;

"Compliant" Oil Company Is Still at Risk;

The Impossible Task: Replacing All the Bad Chips;

19 Companies That Specialize in Embedded Chip Solutions;

The Crisis in Manufacturing Will Begin in Late 1999, Says Expert;

New York State Agencies Have Just Started Looking for Bad Chips;

New York State's Huge List of Threatened Chip Systems;

Electrical Industry Journal Warns: This One's the Killer;

Chip Failures That Have Already Taken Place: Examples;
Factory Systems Are Being Ignored;
British Firms: One-Third Have Completed Audit
90% of Chips Go Into Embedded Systems;
Y2K Will Kill Patients in Third World Hospitals;
Deadline: 9-9-99;
50% to 80% Chance That Safety Systems Will Fail, Says Report;
Water Systems at Risk: Electronically Frozen Valves;
Health Care Industry: Life and Death;
Minnesota Acknowledges That a Breakdown Is Possible;
Three Myths About Embedded Chips;
Prototype of Machine That Will Test Embedded Chips;
25 Billion Chips; $2.4 Trillion to Fix?;
Self-Defense Against Lawyers, and Let Civilization Collapse!;
80% of Problem Is Here;
Mainline Media Report: 500 Million Bad Chips;
Old PC's Run Large Manufacturing Plants;
Water and Sewer Systems at Risk;
Washington State and Embedded Chips;
The Threat to the Energy Industry: Oil;
94% of Firms Haven't Checked for Embedded Chip Problems;
Florida Power & Light: Bad News;
Empty High Rise Buildings;
Energy Industry: Only 30% Remediation of Bad Chips by 2000;
30 Tests Per Repaired System;
Tall Buildings, Shorthanded Repair Teams;
Unreplaceable Chips Threaten Manufacturing Businesses;
Companies Fail to Warn Clients;
You Can't Test Noncompliant Chips: Shutdown.

The message is slowly getting through to some government

and business leaders. The former head of Britain's Action2000 has called representatives of major public services to meet to draw up contingency plans for 2000. "Our objective is that the Government should be able to say that there will be no material disruption to public services," said Don Cruickshank. There will be representatives from the telecommunications, transport, energy and water industries, as well as from the social services, local authorities, and health and emergency services. The workshop will focus on what each organization is doing about its own contingency planning, and how they can prevent mutual dependencies from compromising those plans.

What this means is that these leaders understand that they need some kind of coordinated manual backup system for their chip systems. One of the more painful realizations coming out of these meetings is that some of the chip systems simply do not allow for manual override.

On May 23, 1998, the London Telegraph put it even more clearly: *England*

"It is now too late to fix the Millennium computer bug and urgent contingency plans are needed to limit damage to the national infrastructure, the head of a former Government advisory body said yesterday. On the eve of a speech by Tony Blair on Government proposals to tackle the Millennium bug, Robin Guenier, who was the head of Taskforce 2000 under the former Tory government, said that a satisfactory outcome was now impossible. He said that correcting the bug was even more complex than originally thought and most companies had made no preparations. Gwynneth Flower, the director of Action 2000, set up by the Labour Government to advise on the bug, has said that it is "a problem that could bring down a government".

"With only 20 months until 2000, only 16 per cent of

public sector companies have started to convert software. . . .

"Mr. Guenier said that, despite widespread warnings, business, industry and the Government had failed to take the issue seriously. "Significant numbers of large companies do not have it under control," he said. It is, put quite simply, "[not] inconvenience [but] disaster." Mr. Guenier called on the Government to "unambiguously confirm that we are now dealing with an emergency" and draw up appropriate contingency plans...

"Mr. Guenier urged the Government to insist that the chief executives of all large utilities provide assurances that there will be no service interruption. Despite repeated requests, none of the water companies will confirm that they have satisfactorily corrected the computer systems that control the supply of water and disposal of sewage. British Telecom has published the measures it is taking to ensure that telephone services work next century, but it cannot guarantee it will be possible to make or receive calls on Jan 1."

CHAPTER 7
What Will Become of Your Family?

*"We could end up with a real catastrophe that
could affect many people's lives around the globe
... One industry expert has called the ... (y2k)
defect 'the most devastating Virus
ever to infect the world's business
and information technology systems.'"*

Washington Post,
September 15, 1996

"I just hope I can keep all my children alive."

This was the 1997 comment of a banker who was asked his
assessment of the Y2K crisis. He understood that his bottom line
concern was not about his bank, his money, his lifestyle or his
career. He saw the threat for what it was and knew he would have
to take unusual measures to keep his young children alive.

His comment is perhaps the most judicious comment of any
I have heard. How many people see the same facts as this banker,
but fail to see reality and fail to come to the proper conclusions?
In the first three years of the crisis, some people will lose children;
some children will lose parents.

By the time you receive this and read it, y2k will be a
household word. Effects of the crisis will be a matter of
significant public discourse. Yet most Americans will be saying,

107

"Aw, shucks. I'm not worried about it. Bill Gates or some other geek will come up with a cool fix in the nick of time."

If you look closely you will notice that even people who jest about the dangers will be taking precautions of some kind. Most of them will be preparing for brief technology glitches, which they estimate will last a day...maybe a week. They will create little stockpiles of bottled water, toilet paper, canned food and, perhaps, coffee.

And you too will be taking precautions of some kind. The precautions you take will reflect your opinion about how long the recovery will take. If your precautions will see you through three or four months of hardship, what will happen to you if the crisis lasts three or four years? Please form your opinion very carefully.

Remember that some of the confident people installed as "year 2000 project managers" were forced to admit after months at the job that they were totally unprepared for the job, totally overwhelmed by the task and have no idea how to finish it on time. In the summer of 1998 some of the better project managers, who started repair efforts as early as 1994 had to admit that their efforts were not going anywhere and that they needed to start over. Remember that some of the smartest veteran programmers have been completely bamboozled by intricacies in the programs they need to fix. Remember that other capable programmers are astonished by the ways their simple fixes in one line of code mess up other lines of code. And most of all remember that dozens of programmers have inferred publicly that they simply don't have time to finish the job properly.

Think hard about what this will do to your family and take the steps now to get them as far away from the effects of Y2K as possible. The steps must be taken early. There are no steps that can be taken once the crisis begins.

If you wait until the crisis develops, you may fall into a statistical category of person who has a very difficult time staying alive. That is the "refugee" category. Refugees are people who have but one high-risk option for survival, and that is to wander from unsafe places in search of safer places. Even the very wealthy, if they have no access to their wealth, can be thrown into this category.

Increase your options now by planning early for the three worst threats. Listed in order of greater risk, they are

1. Disease

The threat of disease will arise mostly from shortages of clean water. Solutions are to acquire portable water purification gear or, preferably, an independently powered remote rural well. Which means you must move to a rural location. Additionally, you must acquire proper stores of medication that may not be available from current providers.

2. Malnutrition

Food shortages could be serious and lengthy. Obtain as many supplies as possible, and store them in a safe rural retreat.

3. Violence

The targeted victims of violence will be those who have taken precautions to prepare for threats one and two. Your options for resistance are outlined briefly in Appendix E.

CHAPTER 8
Editor's Official Prediction

"If today were Jan. 1, 2000,
and your computer systems were in the shape they are today,
Baton Rouge would come to a halt.
It wouldn't come to a grinding halt, it would snap to a
halt because the systems we depend on will not work."

Peter DeJager
From a speech to
Baton Rouge business leaders,
June 12, 1998

Most readers bought this book to find out what shape computers will be in by the deadline. The prognosis is not encouraging. The good news is that by December, 1999, America's computer professionals will finally have a good picture of where our computers stand and what must be done to fix them. The bad news is that the computers won't be ready and it will be too late to fix them. Today we have only a glimpse of how vulnerable our computers are and how dangerous the millennium bug really is. Our understanding of the problem is so inadequate that there are people today who still believe it is possible to make every system and every computer compliant and compatible by the deadline. It is not possible. Most of the world passed the "too late" marker in 1995. America passed it in 1997. It's too late to be ready. Every time we get a more accurate, revealing look at the problem we encounter more bad news. This does not mean that the repair efforts should stop. As long as electricity is available, it would be good to continue the process, even into the 21st century. It teaches us more about what we must do to recover from the damage done on January 1, 2000.

What matters in the following prediction is not what this editor predicts, but what you predict will happen. You will act on what you believe. How will the damage affect you? My prediction, offered here as the best compilation of professional assessments, is based on an 18-month study of the likeliest scenarios, and reduced to language we can all understand.

Summary: *Because our civilization waited too late to begin the y2k repair process, every developed nation will fall into a seven-to-eight-year economic collapse followed by a slow, delayed, awkward recovery. Computer professionals will continue to make heroic efforts to get hardware and software ready for 2000. By the third quarter of 1999, many project leaders, including those with electric utilities, railroads and government services will admit defeat, and will brace for the worst. The only families likely to be untouched by y2k are some geographically remote Mennonite and Amish farm households, and those urban families who prepared themselves to live independently of computer technology in rural locations. Every other family will be touched by loss of income and serious local disturbances in services, utilities, the economy, and the fiber of society. Families who are unprepared will be at risk for hunger, disease and lasting hardship. Fear of the future will increase every year until some light is seen at the end of the tunnel in 2006.*

A survey conducted in June, 1998 by the Information Technology Association of America (ITAA) indicates that the more affluent the American, the slower they are to grasp the potential threats y2k brings to their lifestyles.

I predict that serious y2k computer ambushes will begin surprising Americans in mid-1999, causing even the affluent to acknowledge the severity of the situation. I predict that the majority of Americans will finally come to grips with urban and suburban vulnerability by early September, as a number of computer systems begin to falter, causing an economic uncertainty that results in a drastic correction in the stock market (by the end of September, 1999), and the closing of some banks. The closing of some nuclear power plants in October will quickly increase apprehension. I believe this will be seen in the population as a palpable uneasiness, but not as a panic. The press will call it panic, but the word "panic" should be reserved for what happens in January, 2000. Even moderate y2k breakdowns at that time would mean the end of American lifestyles as we know them because of the domino effect on other services and businesses. Any three strategic breakdowns, even moderate ones, could cause ultimate economic collapse. (I define 'collapse' as as a cessation of all economic activity except street transactions; and a suspension of division-of-labor economics. This is a condition which requires families to produce for themselves the things they once depended on others to produce for them.)

I predict that y2k will not be moderate by any definition, largely because of failures of electrical power. In urban North America, in the year 2000, a small percentage of people will die from cold, another percentage will die from hunger, and a yet larger percentage, perhaps as high as three percent, will die from crime and disease. (That percentage will rise in 2001 and again in 2002.) Most y2k victims will be refugees who are attempting to flee anarchical conditions in the cities. An additional, unknown percentage will die from what will be known as industrial disasters

- mechanical breakdowns, chemical leaks, and failures of medical facilities. Suicide will claim another small percentage of people who cannot or will not face the fact they will be required to get a life in the real world. In the real world (a place where many Americans do not presently live) people must live courageous, resourceful lives.

A very early estimate from the Gartner Group was that 3% to 5% of US businesses will be fatally impacted by the year 2000 problem. Failures as few as 3% could be the force that topples the first economic domino, causing many more businesses to die. That 3% to 5% estimate will undoubtedly rise, just as Dr. Yardeni's estimates of global recession have risen from small percentages to 100%. Yardeni is the chief economist at Deutsche Morgen Grenfell. He is a highly respected analyst whose predictions are watched closely by the financial community. A late 1997 estimate from the Gartner Group's research director Matt Hotle looked like this: "We're projecting 30 percent (of organizations) will have mission-critical system failures."

H. Rubin, the Hunter College economist, estimates that 2 out of 3 large U.S. companies did not have a plan to deal with Y2K as of December of 1997. October 1997 was the drop-dead deadline for beginning a y2k repair process that could be completed on time. Will the one-third of large business who began the repair make it in time? Even if they did, they admit that they may still go out of business because their smaller suppliers failed to get ready. According to the Gallup organization, 75% of small businesses have done nothing to prepare for y2k.

Many U.S. insurance companies are calculating the high risk of widespread business failure and are now concluding that they cannot and will not cover y2k-related failures because they will be so massive.

Even if partial electrical power is restored by the summer of 2000, economic implosions will continue, and Americans will think the economy cannot get worse, but it will continue to melt down.

Thus it is not unreasonable to project that, by April, 2000, *at least seven out of every ten Americans will lose their jobs or their present level of income.* Of those seven, one will be able to find clerical work for meager or if-come salary in businesses that attempt to keep going with manual solutions to the y2k disaster; one will be able to find temporary work in agriculturally related services; and the rest will be on their own. There will be no unemployment payments or benefits available. If the power crisis lasts into May, 2000, then the unemployment rate could rise higher than 55%. America has never seen that much unemployment except in specific geographic locations. If the electrical power shortage continues into July, 2000, unemployment will be higher yet.

Can the U.S. survive a 60-80% unemployment rate? Yes, if those unemployed persons fall back on the same small-scale agricultural remedies that pulled America through the Great Depression, and if they don't plan to lean on "New Deal-type" workfare programs. But in the first ten years of the 21st century America will have to be even more resourceful than America was in the 1930s. During that Depression, there were not widespread blackouts of electrical power or sudden shortages of clean water. Even though many families became homeless when mortgages were foreclosed, unemployment was never more than 28% across the nation.

The U.S. government, if it can still communicate beyond Washington, DC, in early 2000, will find it necessary to impose martial law in some areas, and may announce it for the entire nation. Because the threat of compromised communication in January 2000, martial law may be imposed in late 1999. This would be a very dangerous development. Some people may be begging the Clinton administration to do this. The nation should never urge any president to do this, and certainly not Mr. Clinton.

The Army War College released an article in their Autumn 1997 Journal that warns us: "Civilian and military leaders need to expect an increase in domestic deployments of US military forces...

"Strategic leaders can take solace in the lessons learned from military participation in domestic disaster relief, for the record indicates that legal niceties or strict construction of prohibited conduct will be a minor concern. The exigencies of the situation seem to overcome legal proscriptions arguably applicable to our soldiers' conduct. Pragmatism appears to prevail when American soldiers help their fellow citizens."

What this means is that y2k might be so bad that none of us should worry too much if soldiers are outlaws, because there will be more good than bad coming from military assistance."Good" will not be defined by the people. An executive order signed by President Clinton in June, 1994 gives the government the authority to confiscate "all forms of energy including petroleum, gas (both natural and electricity)...Farm equipment...and Food resources."

An even more ominous presidential document is Presidential Decision Directive 63, which talks about the National Security implications of keeping the cities under control through direct military control and Commerce Department control. The precise mechanism for control is an "infrastructure protection system."

The document states that "it is preferred that participation by owners and operators in a national infrastructure protection system be voluntary." If you don't volunteer to be controlled, what then?

The effects of martial law will not be comforting. Any positive effects of military "assistance" will be outweighed by the tyrannical effects of arbitrary absolutism.

Based on estimates of current agricultural resources, the federal government will not have handouts of food or medical supplies that last beyond March, 2000, unless there is a 1999 policy of mass confiscation and forced redistribution of the supplies that responsible families have collected.

History will remember the y2k crisis as one of the most traumatic upheavals of civilization ever. Senator Bennett has publicly compared it to Tower of Babel catastrophism. *I predict that future historians will mark the Clinton administration's policies of martial law and food confiscation as a pivotal event in America's survival or demise, depending on how aggressive those policies become.* Aggressive policies could make a bad situation far worse, as we learn from recent history.

During World War II, the Nazi army captured secret Soviet documents that revealed state-of-emergency polices enacted by Stalin. America's military leaders would do well to study the historical record before endorsing similar plans coming from the Clinton White House. Briefly, this was the Soviet situation following Lenin's death in 1924:

Stalin was struggling to consolidate his revolutionary gains in dictatorial power. The heart of Stalin's political machine was an army of urban bureaucrats who were advancing his socialist ambitions. Stalin's opponents were the rural farmers.

Outwardly, Stalin honored these peasant farmers as the embodiment of the working man, on whose behalf the socialist revolution had come. Inwardly, Stalin hated these farmers because they held the same deep-seated capitalistic values of most hard-working people. The contempt Stalin showed this rural class was not unlike the same impatient contempt President Clinton has shown an American rural class, whose values the White House officially terms "incorrect" and "backward."

Mr. Clinton refers to these agrarians as "rednecks." Mr. Stalin called them "kulaks."

In 1927 there was a famine in Russia. Stalin abruptly decided to use this crisis to cruel political advantage.

There was little food in the cities. The farmers also had little food, but they had stored enough grain for themselves and for the next years' planting. Stalin reasoned that if he seized the food from the kulaks, he could keep his bureaucracy alive and "liquidate" the kulaks -- accomplishing both objectives in one policy directive. In January 1928 Stalin sent 30,000 armed party members to begin the process of seizing food and "smashing the kulaks."

The kulaks resisted -- sometimes with pitchforks, sometimes with guns. When they used guns, the Stalin administration called them "terrorists." When armed resistance failed, the kulaks burned their grain, even in the face of famine, rather than surrender it to Stalin. But Stalin knew he could win in the end. As long as he had just enough food for his favorites in the cities, he could create an ongoing, man-made famine that would kill all the kulaks that couldn't be "dealt with" by party workers.

Stalin ordered, "We must strike the kulaks so hard as to prevent them from rising to their feet again.... We must break down the resistance of that class in open battle."

Marxist scholar Kolakowski calls this battle for food confiscation "probably the most massive warlike operation ever conducted by a state against its own citizens."

At the end of the struggle, Stalin triumphed. Very little was planted for the 1928 crop, and grinding famine continued into the mid-1930s. This was famine by government decree. An estimated ten million farmers and their families were killed or starved, and perhaps another ten million deported to prison camps or prison farms.

But as Historian Paul Johnson astutely observes, this was only part of the desolation. Soviet survivors on both sides of this "war" were badly defiled mentally and morally. In the words of a Soviet official, the "mass annihilation of completely defenseless men, women and children" was acclimatizing party members to violence and brute obedience, transforming them into "cogs in some terrible machine."

This could be the fate of America if the remnants of a functioning government bureaucracy attempt to keep that bureaucracy going through martial redistribution of scarce resources.

Even if y2k domino meltdowns might prevent the federal government from taking any action beyond March, 2000, a 1999 food redistribution program could do considerable damage to the country.

After March, 2000, as communications and funding from the federal level disappear, military rule could devolve to the local level, and then local government will be up for grabs. Most local and state governments will be compromised and broke for the same reasons the federal government will be: there will be no taxing mechanism and means with which to pay public servants. Policemen will go unpaid and schools will close. (I predict that public schooling as we know it will not be available for at least eight years. Some parents may organize certain neighborhood schooling arrangements, but all private and home-schooling initiatives will be parent-driven, parent funded, and highly localized.)

When National Guardsmen go home to try to plant backyard gardens in April, 2000, the vacuum of local leadership will be filled by one of two groups: organized crime cartels or organized religious leaders.

Mob leaders are sophisticated exploiters of y2k already, and understand the future quite well. The *New York Post* reports (June 16, 1998) that the FBI has found a mob-controlled y2k firm that sent programmers into big corporations to rewrite code. The new code, however, was channeling corporate funds into mob accounts.

In some rural American towns, responsible church leaders may assume their duty and calling to shepherd the needy, but it would not be wise to plan on that eventuality. Late 20th century Americans, including clergymen, have little experience with courage and have trouble discerning the difference between good and evil. Not all American clergymen resemble the wimpish, selfish characterization popularized by Hollywood. There are some powerfully capable men in some churches, but for most churches the Hollywood caricature is not far off the mark. I believe each community will see otherwise obscure men and women rise to the occasion in heroic ways. Perhaps you will be one of them, organizing your community in some of the same ways your colonial forefathers organized their communities.

Rural populations will not only struggle with personal survival, but with coordinating the sharing of their scarce resources with urban refugees. If rural communities have extra food, then refugees can become productive new members of the community. If there is little food, then rural communities will find themselves at war with needy refugees. Counties lying in close proximity to America's top-ten metropolitan areas could be overrun with as many as 300-400,000 refugees by June, 2000.

Families who have established themselves for remote (at least 200 miles from big metro areas), self-sufficient living will have good chances of surviving and enjoying rich, family-centered adventures.

I believe families thus situated will be in the best positions to contribute to the rebuilding of American culture, politics, society and technology. I believe the energy and initiative that will lead America back to normality will come out of rural areas largely because urban centers of business will be dysfunctional at best, and completely deserted at worst. Because of the extent of urban and suburban breakdown, I think rural areas will also be the places where humanitarian, charitable and educational efforts will have the greatest potential for effectiveness.

What you must understand about this grim prediction is that it is not just one man's imaginative hunch. Any student who digs into the realities of the y2k problem can see unprecedented disasters on the horizon, that is, if they search in the right places for the answers.

Some computer professionals, who say, 'professionalism will triumph over any deadline,' mislead the genuine student. Among those who should not be trusted as experts are

overworked code jockeys who don't have time to study the big picture.

bureaucrats who have narrowly defined job descriptions

trade magazine editors who write only occasionally about y2k and who have fiduciary connections to industry advertisers

y2k tool salesgroups

On the other hand, it is safer to trust the following professionals:

Computer programming veterans who audit the work of code jockeys

y2k authors who have researched the big picture for more than 18 months

IT managers who have monitored a <u>testing</u> effort for more than two months.

Dan Looper is the y2k manager for one of the nation's most respected auditing firms. He audits the work of companies who think they are finished with their y2k repair. He was asked in June, 1998 if there were any companies anywhere in the US who were ready. There are none. Their "finished" code is riddled with problems. As for compliance, "It's just a dream," Looper said.

The testing stage and the auditing stage is where the reality of the situation is to be found. The repaired code is not passing the tests. The chips in the hardware are not passing the tests.

Since most testing procedures take 18-24 months, many y2k repair projects entered the "hopeless" category in June of 1998.

Any skeptic who listens to the facts can hear his own optimism being ground into pessimism. I've had dozens of conversations with professionals who brush y2k aside with vain fancies like, "If worse comes to worst, we'll just go to manual overrides. Right?"

Well, it sounds like a good alternative...but what's a manual override? Often it's a figment of the professional's imagination, and it's as imaginative as his dream that y2k will be only a bump in the road and not a drive off the cliff.

It's time to listen to those professionals who dig into the questions being raised. For example, is there such a thing as a manual override?

On June 2, 1998, Y2k expert Alan Simpson spoke at a meeting sponsored by the Center for Strategic and International Studies. Simpson has conducted y2k briefings and presentations in over 60 countries, explaining what his digging has uncovered. Simpson was an electronic warfare specialist with Royal Navy Intelligence and a founder of Cambridge Advanced Technology. He bluntly described how interconnected our technology has become.

"Backup generators? Oh, we can use backup power. Problem -- the fuel for the backup power is in the ground in tanks. We cannot pump fuel out of underground tanks. If you don't believe me on this, go around to your local filling station. Ask them to take off the panel and show you where the old crank is. In the old pumps, when the power failed, you pulled up the front panel, stuck in a starter handle, and you could pump for the ambulances and the fire[trucks] -- whatever you wanted. They've taken those out.

"Going back to the rail system, they've taken out manual points. I talked to some of the major rail companies a few days back and said, "Go to manual." And they said, "All our manual points are in the warehouse up in New York State waiting to be disposed of. We cannot switch manually anymore. We have taken out manual reversion systems on most of our key communication, power, and switching systems."

When responsible people understand the facts of our current technological situation, they don't imagine fanciful fixes that can't or don't exist. They begin to think about the implications of reality. The reasoning goes like this:

"So, if the railroads don't have manual overrides, and their computers go down, the trains can't move. And if the trains can't move, the coal-powered electricity plants can only run for six days...that is, if their computer hardware still works. And the grocery stores and factories will have to close for lack of electricity or because they're empty. And if the supermarkets close, and there's no power to pump clean water into the city, then the city can't run...and if the city can't function, the people will have to..."

Techweek Magazine, May 4, 1998, published a summary of some of the conclusions being reached by responsible people. A portion of that story bears repeating:

" 'New York, Chicago, Atlanta, and a dozen other cities are going to resemble Beirut in January 2000. That's why I moved out of NYC to rural New Mexico a couple months ago... The government of the U.S. as we currently know it will fall on 1/1/2000. Period.'

"That's computer programming guru Ed Yourdon talking. And he's one of the more conservative Y2K experts. There's growing alarm in computer programming circles about what is seen as the abysmal failure -- out of hubris or greed or both -- of American business and government to take the Y2K crisis seriously enough.

"Small but significant numbers of concerned citizens, *TechWeek* has learned, are beginning to act on those ominous predictions and are heading for shelter in self defense. They are millennium survivalists, heading for the woods and hills, stocking in supplies, hunkering down, and preparing for what they see as an apocalypse fostered by our total reliance on, and interconnectivity with, flawed computer systems, along with institutional denial of Millennium Bug's threat. None of the mission-critical sectors in the United States are even close to being Y2K compliant, say the experts. Not the 9,000 electric utility plants. Not the 11,000 banks. Not the telecommunications companies. And certainly not the U.S. government, which is way behind in its own Y2K fixes....

"*TechWeek* also spoke with a programmer who works for a Midwestern nuclear power plant with lots of embedded systems. He was a member of a Y2K study team that concluded that plant operation in the year 2000 would be difficult at best, and fixes would cost about $30 million. Plant management axed the proposed fixes. He's now planning to pack up his family ASAP and head out to a small town in the country. Under NRC rules for "unanalyzed situations," the plant will have to be shut down in December 1999 for testing, he believes.

"*Techweek* also interviewed a businesswoman who runs a manufacturing company in Joplin.

"'When I heard about the Y2K risks with embedded chips last year, I wrote to 50 of my suppliers, such as trucking companies and makers of power saws and copy and fax machines,'" she says. 'Except for my insurance company, none of them could certify in writing that their products or services would continue to work in the year 2000. Southern Pacific just sent me a joke poster: 'January 1, 2000: just another day.' ' And without the five trainloads of coal a day, the local power plant in Riverton, Kan., could not provide power.'

"'It became obvious that American Panel might not be able to continue in business,' she says. After trying, unsuccessfully, to sell the company, Turner decided to prepare for the worst—a return to an 1800s lifestyle on her five-acre "hobby" farm.

"'I'm learning how to drive a team of horses with a plow," she says. "I drove 18 miles Saturday. I drove a team of Missouri mules first, then a pair of horses. A good day, except I learned how hard it all is!' she says. 'I wanted to help others deal with 1/1/2000, so I expanded my cooler business to manufacture low-cost $7,000 'Survival Dome' houses.' These 32-foot insulated domes are covered with stones and can be assembled from a kit and heated with a small wood stove."

This is how y2k is shaping up. Students of the crisis are predicting many of the same scenarios. Because they don't want to be vulnerable, they are taking reasonable precautions. Their precautions are creative enough and inventive enough that it gives me great hope that some families will come through y2k just fine, and will take a few others with them through the crisis and over to the other side.

Ken Griffith is a young, single, computer programmer who quit his job in order to organize a rural survival community for a dozen families. He didn't know who those families would be when he started acquiring farmland and subdividing it but, one by one, the families are moving in and preparing for adventure.

Another young man, newly married, just showed me a stack of food staples, eight feet high, he has collected for his widowed mother-in-law and stored in her garage.

People are starting to look out for one another. The legacy of y2k will not be desolation and despair exclusively. Because we have advance warning, some of us will be in a position to assist others in ways that are noble. We will be able to endure the privations in ways that are ingenious. We will be able to handle the unexpected in ways that are resourceful.

Some of the stories that will be told about y2k in years to come will be much more impressive than today's bragging about the power and genius of our modern computers. I believe some of the achievements coming out of the crisis will be more imaginative, bold, and enterprising than any we can now picture.

Without the warning, and without preparation, survival could well have been the mythic curse of world history's most vulnerable time, with death and desolation on every side. But with this warning, and with the resources you can find in the following appendices, you can not only make it, you can make a contribution to the positive legacy of y2k's mark on world history.

CHAPTER 9
Plan of Action Summary

"When I was a kid I always wanted to be a cowboy.
Now that I know I'm going to spend my future in the past
it sounds like a wonderful way to spend my retirement years."

Emmett "Doc" Brown,
Back To The Future III

When a time-machine malfunction forced Doc Brown back to the year 1885, he made the most of it, shoeing horses and fixing wagons and enjoying himself in the Old West. In his spare time he applied what he knew about modern technology to make his life even more enjoyable.

Saying goodbye to your current lifestyle may not be as difficult as you think. You may wince because it looks like you're being forced back into the 19th century. But you're not. You're going into the 21st century with every resource and bit of knowledge you can take with you. Make your decisions by looking at the future, not the past. Evaluate the value of certain goods by determining their value in the future, not the past. Which will be worth more, a '75 Ford pickup or a '99 Mercedes SUV? The non-computerized Ford may be. A $50 hand-cranked grain mill be soon worth five or six times as much as your $2,300 exercise machine. Your brother's old beat-up camping gear will be worth more than the most expensive clothing hanging in your closet. That old hand-cranked washing machine is indeed a relic of the past, but it will have many times more value in 2000 than its current antique value.

If you move now toward a position of financial and physical safety, you may be able to preserve and even improve on the things that are important to you. You can have more time to read, more time with your family, more control over your affairs, more freedom from government intrusions, more direct satisfaction in your daily work...

In fact, if you act now, you can provide your own electricity and have air conditioning, a VCR, an electric milking machine and an electric butter churn...and that's just in your barn. That's right...your barn. Even the most comfortable of alternative living arrangements must account for the role you must play in providing for your basic needs. If you are not providing food for your family in an agrarian setting, there is no guarantee that you will find food available anywhere else at any price.

If you try to keep one foot in today's crumbling world while you're trying to build for your agrarian future, you may not make it. You'll have to approach each of these steps decisively and quickly. Time is fast running out. If you realize now that there is adequate reason to act to protect your family from very real potential danger, the following steps should help you stay on track as you move toward a new way to live. These steps were compiled for urbanites. Farmers will know how to modify these steps for their own strategy of preparation.

1. Sell your mutual funds now. If you're concerned about losing your stock market momentum for long-term investment, remember that it took the stock market sixty five years to come back up to break-even after the 1929 crash, and that the 1999 crash recovery may be much longer than that. If 55% of your

proceeds can get you entirely out of debt, spend them. If not, concentrate all your liquid assets on the following steps, and try to sell your urban real estate to raise more.

2. Sell off unneeded luxury possessions to raise yet additional cash. You will need cash to purchase the items you see listed in the Appendices. Keep your tools. (Remember, the value of luxury items will drop. If you "need" those items later, you can buy them for a song in 2001.) Put the proceeds in your local bank if you're reading this before March 1999.

3. With 30% of your savings, purchase gold and silver coins. Keep them in a safe place at home, not in a bank safe deposit box, or at the dealer's location.

4. If you are one of those 180 million Americans who claims to be a church member, find out if your church is planning a ministry strategy that adresses a six-year period of economic collapse and refugee relocation. If you think the plan is comprehensive, stay and help. If the plan is not, g*o immediately to step 5.*

5. Locate a place you can stay outside the city. If you buy, don't pay too much. Be creative and get something within your budget so that you don't have to borrow money. If you must buy, spend up to 50% of what you have in the bank. This is the most important thing you will buy. If you can save your money and negotiate a lease or sharecrop arrangement with a farmer, do that. Make sure your rural retreat has an independent water supply and a soil suitable for gardening. Prepare it for winter habitation. Install a wood burning stove and load up on lots of firewood or

coal.

6. Stock your new country place with food supplies, and the other items on the lists in this book. Pay special attention to the medical items, water purification gear, grain, and non-hybrid seeds. Your goal should be to acquire three full years' supply.

7. Make sure you don't put off step 6. All these items will become scarce in 1999, and will begin to disappear quickly in May 1999. After completing step 6, if you have the time and money, install generator, hydro-, or solar electricity.

8. Move your gold and silver supply to your country place. Be creative about where you hide it. You should also hide a hard copy of all your important records, deeds, insurance policies, and records of anything else you haven't sold.

9. Buy a gun, plenty of the proper ammunition, and learn how to use the gun safely. At a minimum you should own a shotgun and a deer rifle. If you're not sure you would ever use the gun, buy it now anyway and contemplate defense and hunting ethics later.

10. If possible, sell your home in the city or suburb and invest the equity in your country holdings. Acquire extra food for needy refugees you may be able to help.

11. Affiliate yourself with a good local church near your country place, especially if you're a skeptic who never had time for God. This goes double if you never had time for church.

12. Explain the y2k situation to the pastor, urge him to prepare

his congregation so they can work together to care for one another. You and everyone in your surrounding community will need each other. Photocopy Appendix J and give it to church leaders, or pass around copies of this book.

13. By April, 1999, remove all your remaining savings from your local bank and convert 80% to gold and silver coins. Keep 20% as cash, preferably US$20 bills or clad coins. If it hasn't become illegal to do so, you must cash out your IRAs, 401Ks or other retirement funds if you ever expect to benefit from those funds.

14. If you haven't quit your city job, and if you haven't sold your city property, be sure you have a pre-1980 automobile that can get you to your country place. If your employer is still in business by November, 1999, make arrangements with your boss to be gone from work from Thanksgiving 1999 through the second week of the New Year. Don't plan to go back into the city for anything during this period. If power goes off in your city, your job will be dead and long gone. If power is rationed, and your company is still in business after January 10, and can pay you, you can decide at that point what to do about your job. Even if there is electricity in your city, there is a better than 40% chance that your business will be closed and a 60% chance that it will fold by April, 2000. If it dies, you will be very thankful that you were prepared to be able to do without your job, and are safely located in the country.

Because of the unrest and uncertainty of the first quarter of 2000, it will be necessary for you to stay home -- in your new home. Stay put. Even if travel is possible, it will not be advisable. Plan to stay close to your homestead through the spring planting season. A most profitable pastime would be the reading of Carla Emery's book T*he Encyclopedia of Country Living.* *B*uy the Ninth Edition from Sasquatch Books for $27.95 at (206) 467-4300. This is a priority purchase.

The food and fuel you stored will get you through the winter, and beyond, if you followed the recommendations in the Appendices. The gold, silver and cash you put back should appreciate over the winter by 100-1200%, and may last you through many more months of rough times.

15. Thank God that He led you, through these steps, to a place of safety.

A word to the wise: don't try to warn everyone about Y2K. Don't tell everyone what you're thinking of doing for y2k survival and expect to get verbal encouragement from them before you act. Make your decisions based on the facts and then prepare quietly and consistently. If you're worried about loved ones, especially senior citizens who simply would never move to safety, don't nag them about y2k. Rather, prepare enough space for them to join you in 2000, and invite them to spend Thanksgiving or Christmas 1999 at your country retreat. By then they will be convinced and thankful beyond words that you looked after their interests, and will stay as long as the crisis lasts.

APPENDIX A
A LETTER TO MRS. SMITHWICK

Susan Smithwick is a young mom who is living her dream. She's just had her first child, just moved into her first home, and her husband's job is going well enough that she can stay home and be exactly what she always wanted to be: a homemaker. She's an exceptional homemaker, too. With all her heart and soul, she's really in her element.

Her husband recently wrote to me, "My wife won't believe me about this y2k stuff. She doesn't want to face the possibility that my job may end and that we may need to clear out of the city long before that. What's even harder for her to imagine is that our comfortable life might have to be replaced with a more rigorous, unfamiliar life. Can you please ask your wife to write her a woman-to-woman-type letter?" I told him, "Sure, but keep in mind that you're the head of the home and you must lead her and protect her. You see the danger and want to move. Even if she resists you every step of the way, and you stay put and suffer, she will correctly blame you for all the hardships if you give in to her wishes and your family is caught in the chaos and urban crisis.

There is one thing worse than leaving your home, and that's wishing you had left your home."

The following is a copy of my wife's letter to Susan.

Dear Susan:

It's a shame that so few American women aspire to homemaking

133

with the same creativity and dedication you do. You're a great example. It's no wonder your main desire is to settle into and enjoy the nest you have made for your family. Your home is special because it's really homey.

I think it's especially tragic that today, when your nesting urge is strongest, you have to think about uprooting your family and moving to some unknown location. The reason it's hard to contemplate the move is because it's not easy to see the harm in staying.

The y2k problem is especially frustrating because none of us can see the "millennium bug." We have to imagine what it can do to our families. That task is harder today than it has been for any of the families that faced much more visible 20th century threats.

In the late 19th century, for example, it was evident to some of the families living in Armenia that times were going to be tough. They were stuck between two hostile nations, Turkey and Russia. The Turkish government was harsh on the Armenians, and a few Armenian families had the foresight to protect themselves from conditions that were indeed predictable. Prior to 1894, they had the opportunity to move. In 1894 that opportunity ended. The Turkish government decided to wipe out all Armenians, and hundreds of thousands were deliberately slaughtered. The surviving families were rounded up during WWI and forced into the desert. One million died from thirst, starvation or murder by desert tribesmen.

In another example of pending genocide, German Jews were warned early by Hitler's government to get out of the country. Many comfortable Jewish families simply couldn't bring themselves to leave, convincing themselves that no modern government, especially an enlightened, 20th Century German government, would enact vindictive policies toward a part of the population that was so valuable to the nation. Some Jews stayed because Germany was "home"; their roots were there. They lost both their homes and their lives. But other families were willing to pack up and leave

134

the country and homes they loved, because "family" was more important than "home." Those families survived and endure to this day.

One famous family who could see the threat to their freedom and survival were the Von Trapps of Austria. They were not Jews, but they dared to imagine that the Third Reich might live up to its potential. Their story, a true story, was popularized in the film "The Sound of Music." Maria had just married the man she loved and now had the chance to be mistress of one of the grandest mansions of Austria. But a dictator in neighboring Germany posed a threat to her family's freedom and well being. If they left their home it would be confiscated. They would have no place to go. No means of earning a living. But simply being free and together was a higher priority to Maria than staying comfortable on her new physical estate. She understood that she had a more valuable estate in her children than in her physical property.

That family ordered their priorities correctly. They fled Austria with nothing but the clothes on their backs and what little they could carry in their hands over the mountains. They traveled to America to start over, but earning a living was very difficult. They tried singing, but there was not a market for Austrian songs. They tried farming, but they had never farmed. As European aristocrats they had never done any physical work and their new lifestyle was shameful to them as well as nearly impracticable.

But they were together, and they survived with their freedom intact, and with their family traditions secure. History proved that they did the right thing. Had they stayed they would likely have been among the Catholics who perished in concentration camps.

Why do some people see potential danger and some not? I don't know. But those who do see danger seem to share this character quality: they don't take the little things for granted, because they know the little things are really very big things. Freedom. Food. Water. Electricity.

These things are not to be taken lightly. The most comfortable home becomes something very different without these gifts of Providence.

This is the threat of y2k. If it lives up to its potential, which I believe it will, it can steal these things away from the best of homes. Once you grasp this, and see the value of your future estate, your present home loses its grasp on you. Who wants a home that can become a tomb? You didn't get married to put up beautiful curtains and plant flowers, but to raise upright children and cultivate high purposes in their hearts. If you succeed, you have a mighty estate. Your estate will carry your culture and traditions to many future generations.

Of course, the wealth your family acquires is part of that estate, and you can help your family preserve that too, if you can convert your present home into capital that can get you to safety. If you sell while there is still a market, and while you have time to prepare your new place, your estate will be maintained and preserved. You will be building future strength instead of present pleasantries. There is nothing wrong with present pleasantries, unless they dull your thinking to the point that you entirely lose your family and your future. Don't be like the German Jews who concluded, "I have to believe that a sophisticated leader like Hitler will protect the interests of all his citizens."

Today the equivalent conclusion is, "I have to believe that a country that can put a man on the moon can fix a two-digit computer glitch."

What you believe will dictate your actions. What is the evidence? Is any banking establishment ready for 2000? No. Has any electric utility tested its system and found it to pass the test? No. Y2k lies in ambush as a danger that could take from you everything of value. Y2k means you must redirect your homemaking creativity into securing the future of your family estate. Even if it meant living a few short years without nice curtains, or even nice windows, it might guarantee that your family would not be homeless. The bigger the threat, the bigger the sacrifice you may need to make to avoid the threat. Y2k is a very big threat.

Today there are living descendants of Armenians, German Jews and of the Von Trapp family who live in comfortable homes because their parents were willing to let themselves contemplate life without food, water and freedom. Those parents were willing to postpone domestic pleasantries for the sake of their posterity. Those parents conveyed their families to safety, and their prospering estates stand in stark contrast to the tombstones that stand over their former neighbors.

APPENDIX B
LOCATION, LOCATION, LOCATION

Why must geography be your number one concern? The scenario described by this book makes it seem that the whole world is going down together. Won't every community be crashing and burning simultaneously?

In the developed countries, yes. But even if the world economy collapses, which appears highly likely, there will be areas of the world that don't crash as hard as others. There will be places in which crime will be low, famine brief, disease contained, martial law unnecessary, and where would-be tyrants are little more than amateur hoodlums. You need to know how to recognize such places and get there in time to prepare for 2000.

To simplify this task, just remember that hardships will be worst in urban areas, and least in rural areas.

This simple rule should help you set your sights on the country. Maybe your family still owns the old homeplace in the country. If so, you're at a great advantage. Most of us will have to start from scratch. Ideally, you want to be located at least 100 miles from any cities greater than 100,000 population, and in as secluded a location as possible. The ideal homestead has rich, fertile soil, a creek or stream, some timber, and is sheltered to the north either by trees (called a windbreak) or hills.

It's hard to overemphasize how much the wind and the weather affects your everyday life on a farm. Please notice the deliberate use of the word "farm." You may have no intention of farming, but of simply getting out of the city and storing up enough food to make it through the crisis and then trying to get back to the city. That's perfectly all right, but if you find yourself in the country eating stored food, you will soon want to taste fresh lettuce, tomatoes, fresh peas and some of the other things we take for granted. If the crisis outlasts your food supply you *will* be turning your retreat into a farm. If you do not have four years of food stored (that's 17,500 meals for a family of four) you *will* be turning your retreat into a farm. I understand that, to any lifelong urbanite, the idea of farming is frightening. But rich soil can be inspiring. I know people who would never consider themselves farmers, but each year they live in the country they try new activities. They grow and store large amounts of vegetables, corn, fruits; they build fence; they vaccinate their animals; they help their cattle and sheep give birth when assistance is needed; they put hay in the barn; and they think they are having fun. You don't have to turn into a farmer, but you will probably do some farming on your farm and learn to enjoy it. Look for a place that will make for comfortable farming even if you don't think you will "farm."

A location that is sheltered from the wind can be several degrees warmer in winter, making your life much more comfortable, and possibly meaning the difference between life and death for your livestock.

HOW MUCH LAND?

How much land you need depends on the size of your family, what you intend to raise and the fertility of the soil. Two acres per person would probably be sufficient for vegetarians; additional acreage will be necessary for raising animals and their food: smaller animals like chickens or rabbits would require another acre or so; goats, another 3-5 acres; large numbers of beef or dairy cattle would require much more land and are beyond the scope of the amateur farmer so will not be considered here.

Some experts are advising to go north rather than south; hungry vagrants from the cities will likely go south, homelessness being more tolerable in a warmer place. As in any area, try to choose a farming community, and one with a source of fuel. Trees are scarce in some areas of the Midwest, but some properties have surface coal or even flowing natural gas. Choose quickly and get down to the business of homesteading your new place.

Once a location is established, it is wise to drill a private water well, which is connected to either a hand pump or backup generator power. A **summary** of the advice offered by families who have successfully relocated goes like this:

- take care of your water situation first. Make sure you can get clean water without electricity. If the well is shallow, a freeze-proof hand pump and Katadyn water purifier bucket will give you what you need.

-purchase a generator and enough stockpiled fuel to power the generator for at least two years, and preferably three.

-connect at least one household circuit to the generator so a refrigerator or battery chargers can be hooked up to power for brief periods. If you can afford it, get a kerosene freezer.

-purchase a wood stove that can serve as the primary heat source in times of power outages (remember, pellet stoves require electricity).

-acquire a large supply of firewood, and the tools needed to get more.

-purchase a good deer rifle and a healthy amount of ammunition. There will be a shortage of ammunition. One analyst has predicted that when American dollars become worthless, single rounds of ammo will be used as currency in some communities.

140

-prepare at least one acre of land for tilling.

-buy a selection of non-hybrid seeds.

-acquire stored food staples of

> Salt
> Beans
> Rice
> Powdered Milk
> Honey
> Wheat grinder and wheat
> Peanut Butter
> Canned Goods
> Vitamin C
> Other Vitamins
> Antibiotics

If you can do these things, you will be self sufficient for as long as your supplies hold out. If you invest some time in learning how to hunt game, fish, and grow produce in good soil, you can replenish your supplies as you use them up and share them with others who were not as wise as you were.

APPENDIX C
THE ART OF HOMESTEADING

Wherever you go there are primary requirements for living off the land. In order of importance, these are:

WATER- This is top priority. You must have water on the property; you just can't bring it in. A spring which flows year-round is ideal, otherwise, you need a well outfitted with a windmill and holding tank, or at the very least, with a manual pump. A stream or pond for fishing or livestock would be excellent also.

Several helpful books on water are available from Eureka Resources, P.O. Box 53565, San Jose, CA 95135, including: Waterhole, by Bob Mellin, telling how to dig your own well with hand tools, Wells and Septic Systems, by Max and Charlotte Alth, The Drinking Water Book, by Colin Ingram, and Oasis Greywater Information, by Art Ludwig, covering using your waste water for irrigation.

Ready-Made Resources 1-800-627-3809 carries many water-related products: underground cisterns, above-ground storage tanks, solar water pumps, water filters, water barrels, solar water distillers, **water purifiers** and the following books:

Rainwater Harvesting, by Arnold Pacey

The Home Water Supply, by Stu Campbell

If you simply don't have time to drill a well, get a portable water purifier and keep it with you at all times. Ready-Made Resources and Nitro-Pak both carry a wide selection of water purifiers.

FUEL- This can be brought in but then you aren't self-sufficient. Timber is the obvious choice, it is common and renewable, but must be cut, split, stacked and cured before it is good fuel. Coal and natural gas resources can only be harnessed after advance planning. Solar, hydroelectric and wind-powered applications are more expensive in terms of dollars, (though the prices are going down every day) but cheap in terms of your labor after they are installed.

GOOD SOIL- Poor soil can be amended but it is a lot of work, and this takes time and probably money, if you need many loads of organic matter, for example.

GOOD NEIGHBORS- In the country, people depend on one another in ways that are all but forgotten in cities. You will probably not have any control over who your neighbors are, but try to land in an area where there are many farmers and few people who are dependent on government financial assistance. Farmers are often very generous with their advice and perhaps even tools and seeds and will be an invaluable resource to a tenderfoot homesteader. As always, the best way to find a friend is to be one.

A SECURE DWELLING- Don't be afraid to live in something as simple as a trailer or a pole barn. If you're building a new home look for a south-facing slope and build your house facing south, and with most of the windows on the south side, to take advantage of the sun's southerly position in winter. In the summer, when the sun is more nearly overhead, the sun will not shine in these south windows. It's a perfect setup: you only get the sun and its heat in the winter.

Ideally, you would like a building location at least 57 feet downhill from a spring, to provide adequate water pressure to your house without the need for a pump. Also, remember to avoid low areas which may flood. Building your house out of sight from the road is wise, and don't build your house downwind from your barn.

Ready-Made Resources (1-800-627-3809) has many helpful books on home building:

The Straw Bale House, by Bill Steen

How to Build your own Log Home for Less Than $15,000

The Independent Home, by Michael Potts

Retreats, by G. Lawson Drinkard III

The Passive Solar House

The Solar Electric House, by Steven Strong

The Rammed Earth House

The $50 and Up Underground House Book

The Ultimate Survival Shelters

Take time to organize storage. List the items you'll need to store and put them in their proper places before you start filling the house indiscriminately.

If the property you've found already has a home on it you need to think about how you will be able to heat and light it, if there is no electricity, or gas or oil for the furnace; where your water will come from, and how you will cook and store your food. You need to decide if you will buy a generator and where you will store its fuel. In short, the place may need to be overhauled for 19th Century conveniences like hand pumps for wells, rainwater cisterns and woodburning stoves.

HEATING

Your heating arrangement depends on the fuel you have available, most likely wood. All wood is not created equal, however. There exist elaborate tables showing precisely how many BTUs each kind of wood affords, but for our purposes, it will be sufficient to know that hardwood (from the deciduous trees which lose their leaves in fall, such as oak, ash, beech, locust, maple, etc.) is preferable to softwood (from evergreen trees, such as pine, fir, spruce, etc.)

Softwoods burn less efficiently, meaning they deliver less heat per cord. The other big problem is that when burned, creosote, a product of their incomplete combustion, lines the chimneys. Creosote is the culprit behind most chimney fires. It can be removed, provided you have the proper chimney-cleaning tools, and the self-discipline to do the messy job regularly . It is much easier to burn hardwood, if it is available. Your chimney will still need periodic cleaning, but much less frequently.

Whatever type of wood you have, if you are cutting down a living tree it must be cut at least six months, and preferably a full year, before you plan to burn it, to give it time to dry out or "cure". It is better to to cut trees that are already dead, sparing the living trees, whenever possible.

You can cut your wood green or dry, but wait for cold weather to split it, for it is much easier then, when the wood tends to be more brittle. Your axe will be more brittle too, and prone to chipping, so keep it in a warm place when you're not using it. Try to have your wood under a tarp or roof of some kind for at least a month before you plan to burn it so it will be dry. Wet wood is a chore to burn and delivers less heat.

You will also need kindling to start your fire; dried broken branches, pine cones, corn cobs or birch bark are all good. Short candle stubs are also very helpful, just put them in with the kindling.

Ideally, you keep your fire going from November to March, so you don't have to wrestle with kindling a new fire each day.

The tools you'll need for working up your woodpile are available from:

Harbor Freight Tools 800-423-2567

Northern Tools 800-533-5545

Bailey's Loggers' Supply 800-322-4539

STOVES

With one of the new high-efficiency wood burning stoves you can stoke it up and shut the damper and not have to reload it for up to eight hours. This makes it easy to keep it going day and night. These stoves are definitely worth their high price tags. They also help you squeeze the maximum amount of heat out of your fuel.

The problem with some of them is that they are engineered so that the top doesn't get hot enough to cook on, so you would need some type of wood-burning (or possibly coal or gas-burning) cook stove. New wood and/or coal burning cookstoves are available from Lehman's Non-Electric (330-857-5757) and Cumberland (800-334-4640), but there are lots of old ones gathering dust in basements and barns. You may be able to unearth one through an ad in the classifieds.

Whether you are to burn wood, coal, oil or natural gas, remember to choose heating and cooking stoves that do not require electricity to blow or circulate the heat.

APPENDIX D
WHAT TO PACK

After the year 2000, nonvaluable things, like entertainment centers, will be cheap. But items of value, like hand-powered wheat-grinders, will be exorbitantly expensive. But it may be hard to travel around to buy things, and some things won't be available at all, so plan carefully what you take with you when you retreat to your farm. Think carefully about consumable goods you now use: toilet paper, soap, shampoo, lotion, toothpaste, detergent, antacid pills, cleaning supplies; it would be wise to have a big supply of these things in case they aren't available for three to five years. The same goes for food supplements and medicines. The only luxury item that should be on your priority list is film for your camera.

I add this item because if you pack everything else in this list, you will be in good shape. The y2k crisis is a huge historical event. One historian said it's almost as big as the The Tower of Babel event, which shifted the planet. Y2k will shift the planet too. I believe you will want to document what you see, and I believe you will also want to document, with photographs, your adventure. James Burke said it's a myth that modern Westerners like you and me could survive a technological calamity like this. I think you will be surprised to discover you can explode that myth. I think you will discover that you can do all kinds of resourceful things you never imagined yourself doing. When you find yourself proud of some unusual feat your family has accomplished together, take pictures! Then store your completed rolls of film away in a cool, dark, dry place until such time as photo finishing places are up and running again.

Now begin assembling the other things in this list. Medications, both prescription and non-prescription, plus a well-stocked medicine cabinet will be invaluable. Some doctors are recommending basic surgical equipment and sutures. Get a tetanus shot in September or October 1999 if you haven't had one for a while, and remember that doctor's offices, clinics and some hospitals may be totally shut down for an undetermined period. Our family is getting several pairs of eyeglasses for each family member who needs them. Get at least one good medical manual. The following books on emergency medicine and dentistry are available from Ready Made Resources 800-627-3809.

FIRST AID Books
Where There is No Dentist by Murray Dickson
Survival Childbirth Manual
Where There is No Doctor by David Werner
U.S. Army Special Forces Medical Handbook
Do-it-Yourself Medicine by Ragnar Benson
Ditch Medicine by Hugh Coffee
Medicine for Mountaineering by James Wilkerson, M.D.
Emergency War Surgery U.S. Armed Forces Handbook
Medical Specialist U.S. Army Handbook
Dental Specialist U.S. Army Handbook
Emergency Medical Care for Disaster
Survivalist's Medicine Chest by Ragnar Benson

Survival Medicine by Marilyn Moore

Homeoopathic First-Aid by Marilyn Moore

Baby & Child Emergency First-Aid Handbook :
 Simple Step-By-Step Instructions
for the Most Common Childhood Emergencies,
        by Mitchell J., M.D. Einzig
The Complete Idiot's Guide to First Aid Basics
        by Stephen J. Rosenberg, Karla Dougherty

MEDICAL CHALLENGES

When it comes to protecting your family from the threat of medical problems, remember that you may be totally on your own. Pharmacies and all but the most primitive hospitals may be shut down. Can you make it on your own? For every crisis this side of serious trauma, yes.

The following information is not medical advice. It is a guide to help you discuss your needs with your doctor. The first list of items you should acquire are generally over-the-counter products you'll be glad to have.

The second list contains some prescription items you should ask your doctor to help you assemble legally and responsibly. He will know which items to add to this list that suit your personal situation best. For example, if a family member is a known diabetic, your kit at home should have a glucose or sugar solution. If a member of your family depends on certain daily doses of special medication, or hormone replacement therapy, get extra amounts, at least two years' worth. Ask your Dentist to get you some IRM (immediate restorative material). Without proper treatment, some dental emergencies can be life threatening. Simple cavities and tooth fractures can open wounds which, if infected, can kill even when antibiotics are available. IRM was developed as a temporary fix for these kinds of problems. It turns out that the "temporary" nature of an IRM fix is so good that it can last for years. Best of all, it can be self-applied to clean, dry tooth surfaces. It can prevent pain, disease, tooth loss and death.

Your dentist and doctor should instruct you in the use of the other items in your supply room. Some would be deadly if used improperly. Let me repeat. Some of these drugs and medications would be deadly if used in the wrong dosages for the wrong ailment. Tetracycline, for example, deteriorates and converts to toxic elements when it gets too old. Old tetracycline can damage kidneys, among other organs.

The reason the editors suggest that non-medical people assemble these items for their families is simple: You may have access to a doctor or a nurse during the crisis, but they may not have access to these medical supplies unless they're found in your medicine chest.

Pharmaceutical companies are not ready for y2k. It appears that many would not be able to ship medicines even if transportation was available. What you collect in 1999 may be one of the most complete supplies in your area.

You may also choose to acquire a HAM radio, powered by your solar backup system. Responsible people like you may be able to pass on and/or apply specific medical instructions. You may also be able to put a local doctor on the air from your home to help others.

But you will not be able to treat anyone in your family unless you have a minimal amount of clean, fresh supplies.

Contents for a First Aid Kit, First List

Activated Charcoal (for
 poisoning emergencies)
Adhesive strip bandages -assorted sizes
 Adhesive tape
 Alcohol - rubbing 70%

Alcohol wipes

Antacid

Antibiotic ointment

Baking soda

Calamine lotion

Chemical ice packs

Chemical hot packs

Cotton balls

Cotton swabs

Decongestant tablets & spray

Diarrhea medication

Disposable latex or vinyl gloves

Elastic bandages

Face mask for CPR

First aid guide

Flashlight

Gauze pads - various sizes

Hot-water bottle

Household ammonia

Hydrocortisone cream .5%

Hydrogen Peroxide

Hypoallergenic tape

Ice bag

Insect repellent

Insect sting swabs

Matches

Meat tenderizer (for insect bites)

Moleskin

Needles

Non-adhering dressings [Telfa]

Oil of Cloves

Over-the-counter pain

medication [aspirin]

Paper & pencil

Paper drinking cups

Roller gauzef - self adhering

Safety pins

Salt

Scissors

Soap

Space blanket

Sam splint

Sugar or glucose solution

Syrup of Ipecac

Thermometer - oral & rectal

Tongue blades

Triangular bandages

Tweezers

Waterproof tape

Small Medical Kit, Second List

Combat Dressings
Large gauze dressings
Small gauze squares
Roller Bandages elastic + cotton
(2in/4in/6in)
Triangular Bandages
Band-Aids -assorted sizes and
shapes (i.e. finger tips)
Sleek Tape 1 in. (waterproof,

plastic/elasticated tape)
cotton buds (q-tips, cotton tips)
thermometer (rectal or pacifier
for children)
Chlorhexidine and Cetrimide
(antiseptic) or Povidone-Iodine
Antibacterial Soap
Lignocaine 1% (local anesthetic)
(USA = Lidocaine)
Augmentin (antibiotic) (a broad
spectrum antibiotic)
Acetaminophen (mild analgesic)
Dicolphenic (mod analgesic) (a
nonsteroidal anti-inflammatory)
Oral Rehydration powder
Loperamide (anti-diarrhoeal)
Benedryl &/or Claratyne
(antihistamines, short + long
acting)
Adrenaline auto injector or
Anakit (USA = epinephrine)
Morphine Sulphate (strong pain
killer) if available
Gamma Benzene Hexachloride
(lice/scabies tx)
Clotimoxazole (anti-fungal)
Paramedic scissors
Surgical scissors
Needle holder
Sm curved clamps
Tissue forceps
Scalpel blades
Emergency Obstetric Kit
(includes bulb suction)
Vicryl 2/0 suture material

5ml syringes
20g needles

Oil of cloves (tooth ache)
Emergency dental kit
(commercial preparation)

If you or anyone you know is dependent on medical devices, it is important to contact the

manufacturer and get their assurance - in writing - that the device will function correctly and safely.

Also, speak to the Physician and express your concerns about the devices. Ask the Physician what alternatives there are to electronic or electrical medical devices, or what you can do if the device fails for any reason. Education is really your only option in this area.

Devices that may be affected by y2k include:

infusion pumps in intravenous drips
heart defibrillators
pacemakers
intensive care monitors
MRI's
CT and PET scans
dialysis
chemotherapy and radiation equipment
laboratory, radiology and other diagnostic systems
monitoring and control systems, including environmental and safety equipment

The frail or elderly, people with particular medical problems that may need a caregiver to perform daily tasks, and people with handicaps, must make special plans for their safety in the event Y2K related emergency service failures occur.

Those who have the following conditions may be especially at risk and should take special precautions:

>Acute or chronic respiratory illnesses
>
>Heart ailments
>
>Unstable or juvenile diabetes
>
>Dependence on tube feeding
>
>Epilepsy
>
>Tracheotomies
>
>Urinary catheters
>
>Colostomies
>
>Dialysis – dependence

Your pharmacy maintains its records on computers, as do most businesses. They are subject to the same problems. If you take medication regularly, it's a good idea to ask your doctor to write you an additional prescription ahead of time, to protect you if the pharmacy experiences any problems or delays.

Some problems may be prematurely expired prescriptions, accessing old file information no longer current, changed medication and dosage, etc. They may also "lose" your information, or have trouble processing it with your insurance carrier. Don't forget to bring cash with you when it's time to purchase.

If you are able to receive medication during and immediately after the date change, check your prescription information carefully for : your name, drug name, dosage, quantity, expiration, etc. Errors are still possible, and it's a good habit to practice regardless.

Few doctors are willing to give straightforward advice because of potential lawsuits. Dr. Jane Orient, president of Doctors for Disaster Preparedness, believes in providing information, and has given permission to reprint the following list of supplies. You may contact her organization for additional information or a copy of her newsletter at 275 N. Kimball, Box 272, Tucson, AZ 85719.

Dr. Orient's Basic Medical Recommendations

In putting together your own kit, you will need to take your own family's situation into consideration. And you will need the cooperation of your physician for obtaining prescription drugs. Finally, you will need to consider how much you can afford to spend. Do not buy drugs until the basics—food, water, ventilation, shelter, etc.—are provided. Remember that the human race survived for many centuries without modern medicine, but could not survive more than a few days without water.

In constructing this list, various assumptions are made about the situation. One is that major surgery will not be practical under shelter conditions. This requires highly trained personnel and at least $1000 worth of instruments.

A person with appendicitis would have a better chance with antibiotics and rest—taking nothing by mouth except medications and clear liquids—than with surgery by amateurs.

Many items could be added to the list. For example, persons who know what to do with them might want to store materials for splinting or casting fractures (which could be splinted by expedient means in the absence of such materials). Intravenous solutions—and the means of administering them—might also be stored. Because of expense, space requirements, and the need for some expertise in their use, they are not listed here. Wholesale prices, when available, are given in brackets.

DISINFECTANTS

Betadine scrub (1 pt.) [$2.70] Use for cleansing intact skin—the detergent is very toxic to tissues. Betadine solution (1 pt.) [$2.70]. The solution may be used to cleanse wounds, preferably in a 1:100 dilution (about three drops per ounce of water). With dilution, the tissue toxicity is less, and the concentration of free iodine—the antimicrobial agent—is

WHAT WILL BECOME OF US?

actually greater. Betadine is not suitable for water purification. For that purpose, one can use tincture of iodine, which is 2% iodine and 2% sodium iodide in alcohol, at a concentration of 3-5 drops per quart of clear water or 10 drops per quart of cloudy water. Chlorine bleach (e.g., Clorox)(a 5.25% solution of sodium hypochlorite). Dry pool chlorine, "burn out" or "shock treatment," is 65% calcium hypochlorite. A solution of about the same concentration of hypochlorite as commercial bleach can be made by dissolving about 24.5 grams (about 10 tablespoons) of the powder in one gallon of water. CAUTION: The dry material gives off chlorine gas in small quantities, enough to cause symptoms in some persons. Keep container tightly sealed, and prepare solutions in a well-ventilated area.

For cleaning instruments and surfaces, a dilution of 1:10 is recommended. Such solutions are relatively unstable and should be freshly prepared. Scrub off the blood and body fluids (organic materials react with the chlorine and destroy it), then allow the instrument to soak in the disinfectant. Note that tuberculosis organisms are uniquely resistant to chlorine. Do not use hypochlorite for irrigating wounds (as was done during World War I), because it dissolves blood clots.

ANTISEPTICS

Acetic acid: 5% (1 gallon of household vinegar). This can reduce the microbial count (especially Pseudomonas) in infected wounds. Half-strength vinegar can be used to irrigate the ear in external otitis. Use 3 Tbsp. per quart of water as a douche for vaginal infections. Hydrogen peroxide: 3% solution (1 pt.). Some use peroxide to cleanse wounds. It is helpful as a mouthwash for oral ulcers or Vincent's angina.

DRESSINGS

Band-Aids (2 boxes)
Sanitary napkins. (1 box) to use as pressure dressings.
Gauze pads (4 by 4 inches, 4 packs of 200 each) [$35.00]
Conforming gauze roller bandages-. (4-inch, 12) [$4.70]
Tape (1-inch, 12 rolls) [$12.35]
Ace bandages Get the elastic, 4-inch kind (2).
Safety pins. Box of assorted pins.
Bed sheets. For making triangular bandages or strips
Sewing shears

156

SURGICAL INSTRUMENTS (FOR MINOR WOUND REPAIRS)
Iris scissors 1 curved, 1 straight. [$3.75, $3.45]
Mayo Type scissors One sharp, one rounded blade. [$13.45]
Needle holder [X4-95]
Hemostat (Kelly clamp) [$5.80]
Splinter forceps
Tissue forceps, with teeth [$2.10]
Scalpel handle. (#3) [$6.95]
Scalpel blades (10 each, #10, 11) [$4.70]
Suture needles Assorted (1 dozen 0000 nylon, $13.15)
Reusable needles Obtain from veterinary supplier
Suture material: Catgut from veterinary supplies; cotton and nylon thread

DIAGNOSTIC EQUIPMENT
Thermometers
Sphygmomanometer [$21.75]
Stethoscope Nurse's [$4.50]
Flashlight and extra batteries

OTHER CLINICAL SUPPLIES AND EQUIPMENT
Latex gloves. Box of 100 [$14.95].
Surgical masks Box of 50 [$13.15]. A mask helps protect against airborne infections and would be of some benefit in preventing inhalation of small particles if one needed to go out of doors in fallout conditions.
Syringes 1 box of disposable 3-5 cc syringes and/or several of reusable glass; several 1 cc syringes for administering adrenaline [$11.95/100].
Assorted needles 21- and 25-gauge r7.50 per box of 100].
KYJelly: 2 tubes [$1.90].
Cotton-tipped applicators
Baby ear syringe A rubber bulb useful for suctioning mouth of newborn or for irrigating ears.
Umbilical clamps - strips of clean cloth can substitute.
Plastic oral airways - get assorted sizes [$4.95]. This simple device can keep an unconscious patient from "swallowing his tongue."

Foley catheter set. Kit that includes catheter and drainage bag [$7.50].
Enema bag

157

Notebook, pencils, pens
Soap
Measuring spoons and dropper bottle
Plastic bags

OVER-THE-COUNTER MEDICATIONS

Acetaminophen (Tylenol): 500-mg "extra strength" (1000 tablets) [$13.90].
Acetaminophen liquid for children: 1 bottle. [We are told that infant Acetaminophen is more potent than children's.]
Antacid. (1000 aluminum-magnesium hydroxide tablets) [$5.75].
Antihistamines. Chlorpheniramine 4 mg and/or Diphenhydramine (Benadryl) 25 mg (1000 tablets) [$15.65]. Benadryl is also useful for hives, and of some value for nausea.
Aspirin: 300 mg or 10 gr (1000 tablets) [$9.50].
Kaopectate: Some physicians are skeptical of the value of this time-honored preparation, and recommend Pepto-Bismol instead.
Laxatives. 200 senoxon tablets and 1000 milk of magnesia tablets [$4.40, $6.15]. In small amounts, milk of magnesia can also help to replace magnesium lost if patient has chronic diarrhea.
Petrolatum: (Vaseline, 1 lb.) [$1.80]. This lubricant and emollient is especially good for diaper rash or for making nonadherent dressings.
Pseudoephedrine: 30 mg (1000 tablets) [$7.95]. Give one or two tablets from one to three times daily as a decongestant.
Tolnaftate powder: Tinactin, 45 grams. [$2.10]. Apply from two to three times daily for fungal skin infections.
Zinc oxide. (1 Ib.) [$3.75]. This mild astringent and antiseptic is used in diaper rash and various skin diseases, or as a sunscreen.

From the Grocery Store:
Baking soda is most important for oral fluid replacement (see below). It has been used as an antacid, though it is certainly not ideal. Persons who need to restrict sodium intake should not take soda for an upset stomach.

Coca-Cola syrup [$6.50/gallon]. One consultant suggested this as being surprisingly effective for nausea and vomiting.

Potassium Iodide

To block the thyroid gland to prevent the uptake of radioactive iodine contaminating food and water, take 4 drops of a saturated solution daily. Fill a brown dropper bottle about 60% full with crystals, then add water until bottle is 90% full. Shake. Check to be sure that some crystals remain out of solution. (See Nuclear War Survival Skills, p. 114.)

Prescription Drugs

The following is not intended as a self-treatment guide, but as a guide to choosing drugs for storage. Always seek medical advice before using these potent drugs, all of which have potentially serious side effects, including death. Antibiotics should not be used when they are ineffective and unnecessary (as in viral infections) because of side effects and the risk of selecting out resistant bacteria.

For guidance in determining quantities, the usual duration of treatment for an episode of illness is about 10 days. Adult dosages are given unless otherwise indicated. Abbreviations: bid = twice a day; tid = three times daily; qid = four times daily. Warning: Do not take outdated tetracycline, as kidney damage may result. Always ask the patient whether he is allergic to the drug. If he has a history of hives (an itchy skin rash) or wheezing, or swelling in the mouth or throat, do not give the medication, as a fatal reaction may occur.

Antibiotics
Penicillin: V 500 mg (1000 tablets) [$48.50]. Give 500 mg qid for Streptococcal, pneumococcal infections, anaerobic infections "above the diaphragm" such as abscessed teeth. Although its spectrum is limited, this drug is relatively cheap and causes fewer side effects such as diarrhea and vaginitis.
Amoxicillin: 250 mg (500 capsules) [$40.75]. Give 250 to 500 mg tid for urinary, middle ear, and lower respiratory infection. This is a broader spectrum penicillin. Staphylococci are usually resistant.
Ampicillin or Amoxicillin: For oral suspension 250 mg/tsp. (60 doses) [$15.40]. The suspension is for children who cannot swallow amoxicillin capsules. Give 1/2 to 1 tsp. qid, depending on the size of the child.
Eythromycin Ethylsuccinate 400 mg (500 tablets) [$69.35]. Give two tablets bid for pneumonia or Streptococcal sore throat. The drug is also of

some benefit in Staphylococcal skin infections.

Tetraycline 250 mg (1000 capsules) [$17.70]. Give 250-500 mg qid for plague and various other insect-born infections; urinary infections; bronchitis; infected animal bites, some venereal diseases; Rocky Mountain spotted fever. Avoid this class of drug in pregnant women and young children, if possible. A more expensive drug in this class is doxycycline 100 mg., which is given once daily (twice for severe infections). Doxycycline has fewer gastrointestinal side effects and is better absorbed than tetracycline with food in the stomach, but is more likely to sensitize the skin to sunlight. [Cost is $47 for 500 100-mg tablets; for the higher doses that is $0.18 per day vs. $0.14 per day for tetracycline.]

Oxytetraycline: For intramuscular injection (250 cc. 200 mg/cc) [$24.50 from veterinary supplier]. The dose is about 500 mg bid for severe, life-threatening infections, or 100 mg tid for mild infections, in which case oral treatment is probably preferable. The injectable form may be necessary in patients too ill to take oral medications or for illnesses like plague or anthrax which may be fatal before oral medication is absorbed. Intramuscular injection causes pain; a local anesthetic may be given simultaneously.

Metronidazole (Flagyl): 250 mg (500 tablets) [$21.80]. The usual dose is 500 mg tid, higher for some infections (eg., amebiasis). The drug is effective against certain protozoans including amoebae and Giardia, and for anaerobic bacteria such as those that normally inhabit the bowel and the female genital tract. It can be extremely useful in intra-abdominal, pelvic, and wound infections caused by such bacteria.

Chloramphenicol: The dose is 500 gm qid for anaerobic infections; typhoid and other Salmonella infections; psittacosis; rickettsial infections; or meningitis due to Hemophilus or Meningococcus. This drug is very well absorbed from the gastrointestinal tract and penetrates well into the cerebrospinal fluid (hence its value in meningitis). However, it causes fatal aplastic anemia in about 1 in 50,000 persons treated with it, and some drug companies have stopped manufacturing it. Trimethoprim-sulfamethoxazole DS (Bactrim, Septra): (500 tablets) [$41.15]. Give one double-strength (oS) tablet bid for urinary infections and some types of bacterial diarrhea, or as a back-up drug for sinusitis, bronchitis, ear infections (for resistant organisms or allergic patients).

Others: Some excellent broader-spectrum drugs, especially amoxicillin with clavulanic acid (Augmentin), cefuroxime (Ceftin), and ciprofloxacin are not included solely because of expense.

For Allergic Reactions and Asthma
Adrenalin (epinephrine): For injection (30 cc vial) [$5.55]. Give 0.1 to 0.5 cc of a 1:1000 solution subcutaneously for acute anaphylaxis from a drug or other allergy such as bee sting, or for a severe asthma attack.
Prednisone 5 mg (1000 tablets) [$11.25]. The dosage is variable—usually starting with 40 to 60 mg.—tapering as rapidly as possible. Prednisone is used for severe cases of asthma, poison ivy, sunburn, and allergic reactions, but is not a substitute for epinephrine because the response is not sufficiently rapid. Use with great caution because steroids depress the immune response, among other side effects; however, the drug can be life-saving.
Theophylline preparation (Theodrine): (1000 tablets) [$10.95]. Give 100-300 mg tid or qid, for asthma. Combinations with ephedrine (such as Theodrine), while out of favor these days, may be much cheaper.
Alupent inhaler: [$15.65]. In asthma or acute allergic reaction with wheezing, this has a more rapid action than theophylline.

FOR NAUSEA AND VOMITING
Prochlorperazine (Compazine): 25 mg (100 tablets) [$10.75]. Often used for nausea and vomiting, this drug also may be of some value in acute psychosis. One consultant recommended promethazine (Phenergan) 50 mg instead [$9.00/1000]. Phenergan does not have the additional indication for therapy of psychotic disorders.

FOR PSYCHOLOGICAL DISTRESS
Phenobarbitol: 60 mg (300 tablets) [$11.55]. 30-60 mg is useful as a sedative. The usual anticonvulsant dose is 90 mg daily. CAUTION: Barbiturate addiction is very dangerous; fatal withdrawal reactions have occurred. Haldol: (15 cc vial, 2 mg/cc) [$16.35]. Start with 1 mg intramuscularly for otherwise unmanageable acute psychotic reactions. Monitor the bloodpressure.

FOR PAIN
Xylocaine 1 or 2% (two 50-cc vials) [$6.50]. For local anesthesia.
Acetaminophen with codeine 60 mg (1000 tablets equivalent to Tylenol #4)

[$44.05]. Codeine is both cheaper and more effective for pain relief in combination with Acetaminophen (or aspirin). It also relieves severe cough.

Proparicaine opbthalmic solution: 0.5% (2cc) [$2.25]. 1 to 2 drops will anesthetize the cornea of a patient with a foreign body in his eye. Use only once, to enable you to remove the foreign body. Continued use may allow severe damage to the eye to occur without the patient's awareness.
Nalbuphine hydrochloride (Nubain): (two 10-cc vials, 20 mg/cc) [X29.90]. 10 mg intramuscularly, or more, relieves severe pain. This drug is considered to have less potential for abuse than morphine because it is also a narcotic antagonist (that is, it will cause acute withdrawal in an addict).

FOR HEART AND BLOOD PRESSURE
Hydrochlorthiazide. 50 mg (1000 tablets) [$6.80]. One tablet daily helps to control high blood pressure or congestive heart failure.
Nitroglycerin: 1/150 gr (200 tablets) [$6.30]. One under the tongue as needed relieves angina (heart pain). Lanoxtn (digoxin): 0.25 mg (100 tablets) [$9.10]. Use under physician's advice for certain cardiac conditions such as congestive heart failure or atrial fibrillation with rapid heart rate. The usual maintenance dose is one tablet per day or 1/2 tablet in the elderly.
Atropine 0.5 mg/cc (30 cc) [$1.35]. Because it speeds the heart rate, this drug is useful in some heart attack victims if they have a profound decrease in pulse. More importantly, it is an antidote to many poisons (such as organophosphate insecticides, some poisonous mushrooms, and chemical warfare agents such as tabun and sarin).

MISCELLANEOUS
A year's supply of any prescription drug needed by a family member—rotate each year. This is especially important for drugs with a short shelf life, such as insulin. (Insulin lasts about six months at room temperature, but for only two to six weeks at 80° F.) Immunizations, especially tetanus, should always be kept current. (Tetanus toxoid should be given every ten years. For dirty wounds, a booster may be given if the last dose was more than five years prior to the injury.)

ORAL FLUID REPLACEMENT
Burns. Slightly rounded teaspoon of salt in one qt. of water (the equivalent of half normal, i.e. 0.45% saline). Have victim drink 4 to 8 quarts in first 8

hours (sipping slowly), 4 to 8 quarts in the next 16 hours, then as dictated by thirst.
Cholera or other severe diarrheal illness: To one qt. of water add scant tsp. Lite-Salt (a mixture of sodium and potassium chloride); 10 tsp. sugar; 1/3 tsp. sodium bicarbonate.

BOOKS suggested by Dr. Orient

Cain, Harvey, ed. Emergency Treatment and Management, 7th ed. WB Saunders, 1985
(indispensable).
Emergency War Surgery (first US revision) of The Emergency War Surgery NATO
This completes Dr. Orient's Medical Recommendations

TOOLS

Tools are another thing to pack immediately. Living off the land requires tools of every description; tools for building, tools for cutting and splitting wood, tools for digging, sowing seed, harvesting and threshing crops, tools for shaping and working wood, iron, steel and stone. Plus you need the supplies to maintain, repair and sharpen those tools.

STORED FOOD

The following lists the amount of food necessary to feed one person for one year, of the most basic storage foods, measured in six-gallon storage buckets unless otherwise noted:

Wheat - 5 buckets

Beans -   3 buckets, of various kinds of beans

Brown Rice - 1 bucket

Instant milk - 1 bucket

Rolled oats - 1bucket

Dried corn - 1 bucket

Sugar - 1 bucket, or a comparable amount of honey

Iodized salt - #10 can

Yeast - 36 oz.

Vegetable oil - 1 gallon

Stored food keeps best in a cool, dry location. In the right circumstances the grains and beans can last 40 years. It doesn't have to be stored in buckets, but it must be in containers that are air-tight, insect and rodent proof.

If there is a food co-op near you, contact them about buying food in bulk. For a list of co-ops, see www.prairienet.org/co-op/directory1.html. It may be possible to buy grain directly from an elevator, but you MUST be sure it is grain intended for food, and not seed grain treated with pesticide or preservative. It can be ordered from the following companies also, but shipping will be expensive unless you happen to live close by:

Walton Feed, Inc. 800-847-0465, or at http:/waltonfeed.com

Back Dorr Friends Pantry 712-758-3660

Ready Made Resources 800-627-3809

Noah's Pantry 918-386-2654

Nitro-Pak (800-866-4876) sells bulk foods and also some prepackaged low-moisture or freeze-dried meals in containers. These are no-cook meals that can be eaten right out the container, or mixed with water, reconstituted, and warmed up.

The food on the above list would keep you alive for a year. But it would seem bland to the average American. Add to the above these recommended items, all of which keep well enough for a year or two:

Baking Powder

Baking Soda

Whatever herbs and spices you enjoy

Raisins and dried fruits

Nuts and seeds

Syrup

Peanut butter

Jars of jams and jellies

Cans of fruits, vegetables, sauces

Cocoa powder

Vanilla

Gelatin and pudding mixes

Popcorn

Pancake or biscuit mix

Pasta

Tea or coffee

Vitamins

The items on this list can be bought at any grocery store. Don't put off ordering or buying your food. There is already a six month waiting period at some supply locations.

SEED

Seed companies want you to think that you must buy new seed from them each year, but if stored carefully, seed can last many seasons. If you are not going to plant all the seeds in a packet, take out to the garden only what you plan to plant and leave the rest in storage. Above all, seed must be protected from dampness. Keep it in a cool dry place, in an insect and rodent-proof can or tin, sealed in ziplock bags to minimize exposure to air and dampness.

The following is a list of recommended vegetables; we suggest you grow at least two varieties of each, and if you want to save your own seed, remember to choose non-hybrid (sometimes called "heirloom" or "open-pollinated") varieties:

Asparagus -(grown from roots) for eating fresh and canning
Beans - green: for eating fresh and canning
      - for drying
Beets - for pickling and root cellar storage
Broccoli - for eating fresh and canning
Corn - Sweet, for eating fresh and canning
-Dent, for drying and making into cornmeal
Cabbage - for eating fresh and root cellar storage
Carrots - for eating fresh and root cellar storage
Cucumbers - for eating fresh and pickling
Eggplant - for eating fresh
Garlic - (grown from bulbs) for root cellar storage
Lettuce - for fresh eating
Melons - for fresh eating
Onions - for root cellar storage and pickling
Peas - for fresh eating, canning and drying
Peppers - for fresh eating, drying and pickling
Potatoes - (grown from "eyes")
Pumpkins - for root cellar storage
Rhubarb - (grown from roots) for pies and preserves
Squash - Summer, for fresh eating
      -Winter, for root cellar storage
Tomatoes - for fresh eating and canning
Turnips - for root cellar storage

Strawberries - (grown from roots, avail. in spring)

Note: The plants grown from roots or eyes are only available at their specific planting times, usually in the spring. They can't be ordered in advance and stored. You must plant them when you get them.

Recommended herbs:
Basil
Oregano
Thyme
Rosemary

Grains:
Buckwheat
Oats
Sorghum (for home sugar production)
Sunflower (seeds for snacks or pressing for oil)
Wheat

Also: seeds and beans for sprouting

Alfalfa, mung beans, wheat and other seeds can be sprouted. These make a good source of vitamins and minerals when other fresh greens are not available in winter.

The section on gardening in this book lists many sources of non-hybrid seeds. All of them will carry some of these seeds. Johnny's Selected Seeds (207-437-4301) carries non-hybrid varieties of ALL the items listed above. Shumway's (803-663-9771) sells seed for everything listed except the wheat. They both sell seeds in bulk quantities and also seed for pasturage and silage crops (clover, alfalfa, etc.).

SUPPLIES

You might want to store the following in a large covered plastic storage bins until needed.

Mess kits, or paper cups, plates and plastic utensils (you don't want to waste drinking water washing dishes!)

Disposable baby bottle liners

Flashlight and extra batteries

Nonelectric can opener, utility knife

Matches (a waterproof container is useful as well)

Aluminum foil (better than dirtying pans)

Plastic storage containers

Needles, thread

Medicine dropper

Shut-off wrench, to turn off household gas and water

Candles, lamps and lamp oil

Battery operated smoke alarm

Plastic sheeting (in case of leaks, etc.)

A good supply of containers is

Ropak Corporation
660 S. State College Blvd.
Fullerton, CA. 92631
714-870-9757

SANITATION SUPPLIES

Toilet paper, towelettes (especially for babies)

Soap, liquid detergent (antibacterial soap that doesn't use water is available)

Feminine supplies

Personal hygiene items

Baby needs (diapers, ointments, etc.)

Contact lenses and solution

Denture needs

Extra eyeglasses

Plastic garbage bags, ties, various sizes

> Plastic buckets with tight lids (can be used as makeshift toilets)

Disinfectant

Household chlorine bleach

FOR PETS

> Food (canned and dried)
> Vitamins
> Litter
> Bedding

CLOTHING

What would you buy if you were going on a month-long hiking expedition? Make a list and try to buy those boots (and an extra pair or two), warm clothing, warm coats, and some general work clothing. Imagine what you would be afraid to be without. Get it no later than February, 1999.

APPENDIX E
PROTECTING YOURSELF FROM HARM

When resources become scarce, people will fight for them. Notice I didn't say "quarrel" or "argue." Real-world fights, as opposed to the Hollywood variety, are ugly, violent and unpleasant. Fighters use the strongest force possible so they don't lose. Most of us have never had to resort to fighting to stay alive or to protect our own scarce resources. This kind of confrontation is so unpleasant that many of us may be tempted to conclude that we simply will not fight anyone who wants what we have. We may try to justify ourselves that this is the "ethical" approach, and try to die nobly as we watch marauders carry off our last crust of bread.

This is the issue at hand. If you follow the advice found in this book, sacrificing money and time to be better prepared for Y2K than the next guy, how will you protect yourself if the next guy wants to take what you have? By force? By words? By bribery? Or will you give up without a fight?

In the year 2000 there will be a fascinating explosion of private ethical debate about guns, groceries and gold. This will be healthy as long as the debaters come to the correct conclusions. In the last 2000 years, hardship-driven debaters have turned to the Bible to try to get some ethical bearings. Sometimes they stubbornly turned everywhere else but the Bible, but discussions about real ethics and morality have a way of getting back to the West's primary moral code. But in today's relativistic culture, where public school students have been taught, "there is no absolute moral standard. Who can judge another's ethics? One system is as good as the next, as long as it's sincerely believed..., and the Bible is the root of all kinds of evil...," the Y2K crisis will start with confusing and conflicting standards.

One forgotten history lesson is that non-Biblical systems of ethics don't work. They fall apart when applied to the really tough cases.

If Americans were to begin with Biblical ethics instead of reverting to them too late, how would people behave?

According to scholars who have studied these issues for centuries, the best proven conclusions about the highest standards of right and wrong defense ethics look like this:

1. It is wrong for the head of the household to neglect to provide for dependent family members.

2. God doesn't think it's wrong for one guy to have more than the next guy. Inequality of resources is an ongoing condition that actually serves God's best purposes and often illustrates differences between the obedient and disobedient, the humble and the proud.

3. It is loving to share resources with the less fortunate, but that decision is to be made voluntarily by the lawful owner of the resources, not by governments or thugs who force involuntary sharing. It is best if the sharing follows Biblical standards of stewardship.

"The poor" belong to a special classification of unfortunates and should always receive special attention for charity. However, "the poor" must be properly identified before being given any resources, scarce or plentiful. "The poor" are those who have been made poor through no fault or neglect of their own. They have so few resources they do not know from where their next meal will come.

4. It is wrong to give food to bullies who demand food or to people who do not work.

5. It is right to sell food to the hungry, and is not wrong to sell food

171

to "the poor," or to invite them to work for it. It is wrong, however, to charge interest to the poor for food extended to them on a loan basis.

6. It is permissible and often right to use equal or greater force to defend one's self and one's family from harm, whether direct physical injury or potential starvation.

7. It is not wrong, and is not murder, if attackers intent on murder are killed in the process of threatening harm.

8. If the intruders are merely trespassing, and there is no evidence that they are threatening harm, it is wrong and not justifiable to kill them. Lethal booby traps are not an option for defense because they could kill innocent intruders. Such killings would be classified as murder. However, if the intruders are trespassing at night, and their intentions are not clear, it should be assumed that their intentions are malicious, and it is not murder if they die in your efforts to resist them.

To summarize these eight important points, the Biblically ethical thing to do is to assess the danger of Y2K, put away enough food for your family and some genuinely needy refugees, and to prepare yourself to defend those resources against murderous thieves with whatever force is necessary.

I believe that most American families will come to these conclusions at some point in the crisis. I hope they arrive at these conclusions before, and not after, they lose family members to rape, murder, and starvation.

The way you apply these principles will take judgment and discernment. How much food do you put away? How do you assess the intentions of the gang that's sneaking through the brush toward your cellar door? These are the tough decisions, but they are made infinitely easier if you have addressed the ethical framework through which you will view each decision.

In the year 2000 there will be gangs and individual marauders. Of course, they are around in every city today. In the city of New York, police say they make up about .8% of the population. The number seems higher because many of these offenders are released almost as fast as they are apprehended. In the year 2000 that figure could rise significantly, and their turf will extend far beyond their current neighborhoods. You might call them "land pirates" who take what they can take from those who are vulnerable. If they attack your family they won't be carrying empty shopping bags, but probably shotguns and semi-auto pistols. To stand a chance of protecting your supplies and your loved ones, you will need to match their firepower, and you would increase your chances if you owned greater firepower.

According to military and police experts, both of which know you will not be able to depend on any police protection during the worst of the Y2K crisis, the best firearms for household or farm defense are the Mossberg 590 12ga shotgun, the .223 Remington, the .308 Winchester, and the Colt AR15A2. Simply owning these guns is no guarantee of safety. You must train family members and others to use these safely and then form defense policies. Then practice before your first emergency finds you drowning in adrenalin, confusion and the stress of life-and-death confrontation.

If you are absolutely certain you would never use a deadly weapon, then you must design an impenetrable room into which your family can escape until the bad guys are gone with your property. If the bad guys think you have some stuff in your hideaway room, and they want that too, they may simply besiege you and wait till you have to come out. What if you don't have enough supplies in that room to wait them out?

As you can see, even the pacifist approach to an uncomfortable y2k scenario involves a point at which you might have to confront violent people. At that point you may really want to tell them, "Don't you touch me or my family. If you try, I'll stop you."

How will you do it?

DEFENSE Books

Modern Camouflage by Duncan Long

Total Resistance by Major H. Van Dach

Principles of Personal Defense by Jeff Cooper

Defending Your Retreat

Ragnar's Action Encyclopedia

These, and many other titles are available from:

Nitro-pak 1-888-NITROPAK

Ready-Made Resources 1-800-627-3809

APPENDIX F
YOUR NEW LIFESTYLE

Even if we have made elaborate preparations, and are well-supplied
with all the commodities necessary for life, the total change of life-style we
are talking about may be hard. Really hard.

Devoted watchers of television will suffer, as will those who spend
leisure hours at the computer, and those who frequent malls. For many, it
will be very hard to adapt to a largely stay-at-home lifestyle, probably with
much time spent outdoors, working and sweating. There may be dependent
members of your family (perhaps elderly parents, or teenaged children) who
aren't involved in making the decision to move, who don't really understand

why it is necessary, and who will not adjust well to the sudden disruption of their lives. In times of great stress and turmoil there are always those who can't cope. Some lose interest in living altogether. We must anticipate this situation, evaluate how each member of our families may respond, and make plans to help them.

There will probably be periods of intense activity and other periods of boredom and uncertainty. Because schools will likely be closed for more than three years, it may be the first real chance your children have to get a real education. It's a well established fact that school performance in the U.S. has fallen below that of most other nations. It's also well established that those students who are given the opportunity to be "home-schooled" do very well academically. You can prepare now to offer any student a fascinating course of study at home and find yourself comfortably independent of the public education apparatus. A helpful resource book is *The Great Escape,* which includes a great step-by-step outline for families who want to set up a perfectly legal school operation at home. It's available for $9.95 at 800-771-2147, extension 85.

If the y2k crisis drags on, stay busy, stay productive, and try to enjoy your new lifestyle. Small things can do wonders. For instance, when you buy your garden seed, order flower seed too. Pioneers of a hundred years ago, living in sod houses, and barely scratching out a living from the rough prairie sod, often kept canaries, or potted geraniums. Many immigrants brought seeds or slips of treasured plants when they made their perilous ocean crossings to the New World. They had many other more important things to think about; but they knew, or sensed, that a little beauty, a treasured something from home, would help them cope with the trials they were sure to meet in their new homes.

Music can be a comfort to troubled hearts. A tape or CD player, with favorite recordings, and plenty of stored batteries, might make all the difference to someone you know. Our forbearers made their own music, and if you can play any instrument, be sure to have one. If not, this may be the perfect time to learn, even if it is nothing more than the harmonica (which is actually a very good idea: the harmonica is inexpensive, very portable, and easy to learn.) Song books, too would be useful.

Special edibles are another thing to consider, especially chocolate, which has chemical mood-elevating properties. The smartest way to store it may be in the form of cocoa powder. Its "keeping qualities" are much better than semi-sweet chocolate's, mainly because you can't eat it unless you bake it into something like cake or brownies. There are all sorts of canned goodies, that if carefully hidden will keep quite well: nuts, olives, special coffees, dips...you doubtless know what your family would enjoy.

There is another remedy against despair which was very familiar to our pioneering forbearers, which we would do well to include, and that is the Bible. Probably every family aboard the Mayflower and every family going west on the Overland trail carried one, and took the time to read it, too. Much comfort and strength can be gained from reading those living words, for as the Book itself says, "Man does not live by bread alone, but by every word that proceeds from the mouth of the Father..."

Whether you completely relocate your family or attempt to ride out Y2k where you presently live, you should get to know your neighbors. You will need each other. Find out what each member of the community can do, or likes to do. Try to organize and divvy up certain responsibilities. For example, anticipate hardships like sewer failure and plan ahead on how you can dig community latrines, and where they should be located. Who will pitch in to shovel the dirt? Give thought to how you can work together to preserve your environment. You'll need to work together in dozens of ways to survive well.

If your community or neighborhood is better prepared than most, it will show. You will probably attract refugees from disadvantaged areas. Talk with your neighbors ahead of time about how you will handle any and every challenge you can think of. How many refugees can you accommodate? How and where can they be put to work to be productive? Once your neighborhood reaches capacity, how will you handle new refugees?

APPENDIX G
GROWING CROPS

As soon as you are established in your country home you should start trying to raise your food, even though you may not need to rely on this as your food source yet. Unless you are a very experienced gardener you will need the practice. Don't plan to rely on your first three harvests to supply all your needs. This is why you must have purchased and stored three years of food staples.

WHERE TO LOCATE YOUR GARDEN

Start by considering your sites for gardens, orchards and animals carefully. Contact your county extension agent (look in Appendix G for a state-by-state listing) to help you evaluate your soil, climate and what animals and plants are most likely to thrive in your area. Don't give in to any inclination to figure it out for yourself; you don't have time to make mistakes. Take advantage of other peoples' years of experience: GET ADVICE!

Some plants are very picky about soil type, temperatures and day length, and it is a total waste of time, energy and garden space to try to grow them in the wrong conditions, so don't set your heart on growing any particular thing, watermelons, for instance, until you learn if it is possible where you live. Instead, notice what produce is being grown around you and go for that.

DECIDING WHAT TO GROW

What you decide to plant will also be determined by what you like to eat and how you plan to store it.

FREEZING- Will you be freezing your food? (Only if you have a generator or a gas freezer.) If so, you can easily preserve just about anything, but you will soon run out of room. Good Books on the subject are: The Complete Book of Freezer Cookery by Ann Seranne, and The Blue Ball Book of Freezing and Canning, available from Direct Marketing Dept. P.O. Box 2005, Muncie, IN 47305

CANNING

Nearly any kind of food can be canned also, though it is more time-consuming than freezing. The big advantage to canning food is that once the food is in the jars, no more energy is required except to heat it up, and as the food is already cooked, that is optional. Canning is a lot of work, and requires jars, lids, a big kettle or preferably, a pressure canner, and a good cookstove, but it a good, reliable way to store almost anything you raise, including meats.

Used jars work fine and can usually be found at garage sales or by advertising for them in the classifieds. You will need new lids each year, (don't forget to buy several years' worth of lids) and new rings whenever the old ones get bent or rusty.

Information on canning is available from:

Home Canning Basics, free from the Ball Co. Order from the Alltrista Corp., P.O. Box 2005, Muncie, IN 47307

The Kerr Home Canning Book, Available for $1 from Kerr Glass Manufacturing, Dept. 125, Sand Springs, OK 74o65

There are also numerous University Extension Bulletins on canning, generally priced at 50 cents to $1.50, ask your extension agent .

Our forbearers had neither freezing nor canning available to them, but they managed, largely through drying, smoking, salting their meats, drying beans, grains and fruits, and growing vegetables that could be stored through the winter.

WINTER STORAGE CROPS

Turnips, parsnips and rutabagas have all but disappeared from our supermarkets' produce departments but they were valued in earlier times because if stored carefully, they could keep for months without refrigeration. Other foods in this category are carrots, beets, potatoes, cabbages, pumpkins and winter squash. Certain varieties of apples, too, will keep well into the winter in the right conditions.

A note about potatoes: these are a very important crop for survival. You can grow large quantities of them in a relatively small area, and they keep well. In Ireland a hundred and fifty years ago, many people survived for years on hardly anything besides potatoes.

ROOT CELLARS

These "right conditions" can be met by a cool basement, but a root cellar, with its almost constant levels of temperature and humidity, is much better.

A root cellar need be nothing more than a hole in the ground or side of a hill, dug by hand if necessary, and covered with some sort of board roof over which you have replaced the sod, and which you have fitted with a trap door. The cellar can be as small or large as you wish to dig it, but it should be at least six to eight feet deep, being deeper the further north you are, as it

179

must be below the frost line. It will be much more convenient if it is attached to the house by a tunnel into the basement, and this is almost a necessity in regions where deep snow could make accessing your root cellar very difficult otherwise.

Root vegetables can be stored in bins or baskets, with layers of straw separating the layers of vegetables. As a general rule, you want to prevent the vegetables or fruits touching each other, though if you have vast quantities of potatoes or carrots, this will not be possible.

Only the best produce should be taken to the cellar; and it must be handled carefully. Bruised or damaged food should be used up, not stored. Once your produce is in the cellar, check it regularly for signs of spoilage. Affected food must be removed and what you can't eat can be food for your livestock or compost pile.

The cellar is also an excellent place to keep canned goods and dehydrated foods, provided they are carefully sealed.

More Info on Root Cellaring:

Root Cellaring, by Mike and Nancy Bubel, avail. from Ready-Made Resources 800-627-3809

Cold Storage of Fruits and Vegetables, and

Build Your Own Underground Root Cellar, both published by Storey Communications, Pownal, VT 05261

DRYING OR DEHYDRATING FOOD

Dehydrating food has many advantages; it can be used for all types of vegetables, fruits and meats, (which if properly dried and stored can last up to five years) it is easy, energy-efficient and is the best means of preserving the nutrients in food.

The canning process destroys up to 80% of the nutrients in the food being canned. Up to 40% are destroyed in freezing, but only 5% are lost in dehydration.

The most foolproof means of dehydrating food is with a dehydrator, but it can be done in a warm oven, with the door left ajar to facilitate air circulation, or the old-fashioned way, on screens out in the fresh air and sunshine. Insects and birds live out there though, so you must cover your eatables with a layer of cheesecloth or screen.

The two important factors in drying food are warmth and air circulation, so pick a bright, breezy day for drying, and bring your trays in at night before the air gets damp. It is impossible to dry your food too much, but be sure it is thoroughly dry before packaging, which can be done in jars or ziplock bags.

Ziplock bags are wonderful for storing food, but they are not mouseproof like jars. Bagged foods should be kept in metal bins, like aluminum trashcans, with tight-fitting lids. Leaving a set, baited mousetrap or two around is a good idea wherever you are storing food. Check them often. A few cats around the premises are a great help in keeping down your outdoor mouse population, which in turn reduces the number of mice you get in the house each fall.

MORE INFO on Drying and Dehydrating:

Home Food Dehydration, the Hows , Whats and Whys, by Emma Wheeler

Dry It - You'll Like It!, by Gen MacManiman

Both are available from Ready-made Resources 800-627-3809

The Following titles are all available from Horizon Publishers, P.O. Box 490, Bountiful, UT 84011-0490:

The ABCs of Home Food Dehydration,

New Concepts in Dehydrated Food Cookery

Fun with Fruit Preservation

Home Food Dehydrating

Just Add Water-How to Use Dehydrated Foods and TVP

Food Drying- How to Dehydrate, Store and Use Vegetables, Fruits and Herbs

Food Drying at Home

Dehydrators, both electric and outdoor models, are available from Lehman's Non-Electric Catalog 330-857-5757

YOUR ORCHARD

Once you have decided where everything should go and you're ready to begin being planting, start with your orchard; it will take four-five years before it begins to bear, so get the earliest start you can.

There are three rules to successful planting almost anything:

1. Plant the right plant
2. Plant it in the right place
3. Plant it the right way

We'll look at these rules in reverse order;

The Right Way, for your trees, means in big holes, about three times the size of the rootball, or larger if your soil is very poor. This is hard work, and very time-consuming but will reward you with faster growth, healthier trees and ultimately, more fruit, sooner.

Since you want to put the topsoil you dug up first, into the hole first, pile it up separately when you dig your hole. Mix with your subsoil plenty of aged compost or manure, ground rock phosphate and rock potash.

Trees can be bought bare-root, balled or potted. Each of these must be planted its own way so follow the instructions attached to the tree, or ask

182

the nurseryman's advice. It is very important to plant the tree at the level it has been used to growing, and to plant it standing straight up, or leaning slightly in the direction of the prevailing winds if you live in a windy area.

After planting, your tree should sit in a slight depression like a saucer, about a foot in diameter. To protect your young tree's tasty bark from mice, rabbits, and deer, wrap the trunk with a two-foot piece of wire mesh. Plant full-sized trees about 20' apart, dwarf varieties 10'. If your tree is not self-pollinating you will need to plant another of the same variety near it.

The Right Place for planting your orchard is, ideally, on a slope, which gives the trees the water drainage and air circulation that they need. Avoid windy hilltops and cold, damp hollows. A south-facing slope is best, except for those with frost-sensitive blossoms, which must go on a north slope.

The Right Plants for your area must be chosen carefully. Advice from your local extension agent and neighboring farmers will be your best guide, but this list is a rough guide to what will grow where:

Stone Fruits

Apples- will grow anywhere in the U.S. except the hottest regions.

Cherries- will grow in roughly the same areas as apples.

Peaches- need winter temperatures below 40 degrees to insure winter dormancy, but warm spring temperatures. because the blossoms are very sensitive to frost. They are tricky to grow well, but even a bad home-grown peach is vastly better than one from the supermarket.

Pears- blossoms are less sensitive than peaches', but more so than apples'. Won't grow well where winter temperatures fall below zero. Do well in poor soil.

Plums- Need winter Temperatures below 40 degrees.

NUTS

Almonds- grow under the same conditions as peaches, but blossom about a month earlier, making them very susceptible to spring chill. If you decide to try them, put them on a north slope.

Chinese Chestnut- early-blooming, so plant on north slope. Need several trees for pollination.

Filberts and Hazlenuts- plant on north slope; filberts in warmer climates, hazelnuts where it is colder.

Hickory- plant the shagbark variety for nuts.

Pecan- unlike the trees mentioned above, these prefer the southern half of the country.

Walnuts- grow the Carpathian variety for nuts; very cold-resistant.

Mailorder Nurseries:

Stark Bros. Fruit Trees 800-775-6415

Bear Creek Nursery 509-732-4417

Recommended books on growing fruits, nuts and berries:

The Book of Apples, by Morgan and Richards

The Backyard Orchardist, by Stella Otto

The Backyard Berry Book, by Stella Otto

Pruning Simplified, by Lewis Hill

All Titles available from Bear Creek Nursery

VEGETABLE GARDENING

Choosing the right location for your garden is important.

Some people shift their gardens around from spot to spot, but most serious gardeners choose the best location and work hard to improve the soil year by year, rotating crops within the garden, but never the garden itself. There are many factors to consider: sunlight, water, soil, slope and convenience, to name a few.

SUNLIGHT is absolutely essential. Your crops need, at the very least, six hours of full sunlight per day. There is no way to succeed without it, so you must situate your garden away from buildings which would shade the garden and from trees which would steal sun and water from your crops.

IRRIGATION WATER is the next essential element. Unless you live in an area of the country where you can count on regular rainfall of about an inch a week, you must locate your garden near a water source. Irrigation water doesn't need to be drinkable, which gives you more source options, including ponds, streams, rainwater stored in rain barrels, and "greywater", the undrinkable runoff from your bathing, washing and kitchen cleanup. If you absolutely can't locate your garden anywhere near a water source it is possible to haul water to your garden, but it is hard, time-consuming work and should be avoided if possible.

DRAINAGE/SLOPE is another important consideration. Flat land is the most desirable, but only if there is good drainage. You can't successfully garden where water stands, although there are ways to fix this. The next-best choice is gently sloping land, preferably sloping to the south, with your garden rows planted following the contours of the hill. Steeply sloped land can be farmed too, but great care must be taken to prevent erosion. At the very least, follow the contours of the land, and a better solution may be terracing.

CONVENIENCE is important too. If you are able to situate your garden somewhat near the house you will be better able to keep an eye on it; and it will need constant watching for diseases, weeds, lack of water, readiness for harvest, and for hungry pests, which come in all shapes and sizes.

SOIL fertility is very important, and should be a factor in deciding where to plant your vegetable garden. Just in case you're a real city slicker, you want to look for soil that is dark and easy to dig. The good news is if your soil isn't very good, it can be improved. And if you plan on raising any animals on your place, you'll have a constant and abundant source of one of the best things to use for the purpose.

The first step once you've picked the best garden site is to test your soil and see if and how it needs improvement, or "amendment" as the garden books like to call it. Test kits are available from garden catalogs and stores which sell gardening supplies. Your county extension agent will be able to help here too; call to find out how to arrange testing in your area. If you live in the western part of the U.S. your soil is likely to be alkaline, and need the addition of sulfur. In the East if may be acid, and need lime. Even if the pH is in the neutral range, and your soil ideal, a gardener's best ally is his compost pile, and the sooner you start yours the better.

COMPOSTING

Just about anything organic (meaning, in this case, anything that once lived) can be composted, and the greater the variety of materials, the better. Likely additions include chopped leaves, (run over them a few times with your lawn mower) sawdust, kitchen garbage, (everything from egg shells and tea bags to vegetable and fruit peels) any and all kinds of animal manures, (except cat and dog, which can carry diseases) seaweed (wash the salt off first), wood ashes, grass clippings, nut hulls, animal bedding from the barn, and plant wastes from your garden (like the pea plants once they have quit bearing). Don't put weed seeds in though, or diseased plant material, and if you put in any meat or bones you may invite animals to dig in your compost.

You can just leave your compost in a pile but it does better in a cage,

186

which keeps it from blowing around, and keeps the sides vertical, preventing rain from leaching away the nutrients. In his excellent book, The Victory Garden, James Crockett recommends three bins, side by side, for compost in different stages of decay. The first bin is the one you add new material to. The second is compost that is about halfway rotted, and the third is your most nearly finished compost. Compost is finished when you can't recognize any of the ingredients.

An open-fronted three-bin system can be easily made with seven pallets. (These are usually thrown away by grocery stores or any businesses that receive heavy goods at loading docks. They make good kindling too.)

Make the top of your compost slightly concave, to help water soak in. Compost needs to stay moist to rot, so water the stuff during dry spells. Compost also needs to be stirred up or turned regularly. A pitchfork is the tool of choice for this.

PREPARING TO PLANT

Fall is the best time to till up virgin ground. That way the grass and roots you've turned under can rot over the winter. Tilling can be done by tractor, by rototiller, by a draft animal pulling a plow, or by hand. If you end up doing it by hand, use a garden fork, a sort of short pitchfork with a handle at one end. The deeper you go, turning over and loosening up the soil, the better, down to a depth of two feet if possible. Breaking virgin ground by hand is very hard work. If at all possible, use mechanical means when you plow up sod for the first time, and if the area you will be plowing is over an acre, you'd better count on using something more than man power afterwards, too.

In the spring, as early as the soil is dry enough to work, spread your compost and any other amendments on and then till again. Break up clods with a hoe, remove any rocks, smooth with a rake and it's ready to plant. But if you're willing to invest a little more time and labor, you can spare yourself many longs hours of weeding and watering later by building your soil into raised beds and covering them with sheets of black plastic, first.

BUILDING PLASTIC-COVERED RAISED BEDS

After your garden plot is tilled and ready, measure it off and mark it with sticks and string into rows three feet wide, with two-foot paths in between. These dimensions can be changed to fit your needs, but this is a good, handy size. Make paths to dissect the rows, too, about every eight feet.

Next, dig all the loose, enriched soil from the paths, clear down to the hardpan, and pile it onto the garden rows, shaping them into neat, regular, flat-topped rectangles. Once you've built your soft dirt into beds DO NOT EVER STEP ON IT! You want the dirt in these beds to stay soft and light. If you are careful, you may never have to till this dirt again. Whatever work they require will be easily done by hand. This is one of the advantages of the raised-bed system. It is more work, initially, but much less work in subsequent years. This is the garden system to use if you may not have access to rototillers or tractors in the future, but you do now.

IRRIGATING YOUR RAISED BEDS

Before you cover the beds with the plastic, consider running soaker hoses down the length of each bed, unless you can count on getting about an inch of rain a week. This will really conserve water, and simplify watering, too, especially if you set up each soaker hose and your water hose with special adapters so they can snap together quickly instead of screwing together. This will make it quick and easy to change your water hose from bed to bed, as needed. These adapters are available at any stores that sell gardening supplies, are inexpensive, and will save you lots of frustration.

COVERING THE BEDS

Black or clear plastic is available from any hardware store. Thicker is more expensive, but may last longer than one season, making it cheaper in the long run. You'll need to buy enough for three years. It needs to be two feet wider and longer than the bed you are covering, so you can bury the foot of extra plastic on each side. You probably won't find it in the exact sizes you need but you can easily cut it down to size. It's a shame to use your good, enriched soil to cover the edges of the plastic (which become part of your path), so use gravel, bark chips, shale, or inferior subsoil. (The latter will make muddy paths, but this can be remedied by spreading a thick layer of straw on top.) Bury the plastic along one edge, then stretch it tight and have someone hold it in place while you bury the other side. If the edges are buried well, the wind will go right over the plastic without blowing it away.

PLANTING YOUR CROPS

When you are ready to plant, cut three-inch square holes in your plastic and plant your seeds or seedlings in the moist, warm dirt below, following the directions for spacing your plants that come with the seed. The plastic helps warm the soil, making it possible for you to plant earlier (though not before the last frost date for most varieties).

PLANTS TO PLANT IN PLASTIC-COVERED BEDS

Many crops just won't grow until the soil warms up, and this system is perfect for those heat-lovers. Tomatoes are in this category, as are cucumbers, squash, melons, eggplant, peppers, okra and beans.

PLANTS TO PLANT IN COOL SOIL

There are, however some plants that do not appreciate warm soil, but do better in cool conditions. They include the brassicas, (cabbage, broccoli, Brussels sprouts, cauliflower) most kinds of lettuces, peas and the root crops (potatoes, carrots, beets, turnips, etc.) Do not try to grow them under plastic, but cover their raised beds with mulch instead, to keep down weeds and conserve soil moisture.

ROTATE YOUR CROPS

189

Plants grown from non-hybrid seeds are less resistant to some diseases and viruses than the hybrid varieties, so you should be extra careful to rotate crops to different areas of the garden each year, in case your soil becomes infected with disease-causing pathogens. Crop rotation also helps prevent depletion of your soil's nutrients. You should keep a garden journal to keep track of what was planted where. You may think you'll remember where everything was planted each year, but you won't.

By this point you need to have decided what, and how much of it, you're going to plant, have bought your seed, and possibly have started some seedlings indoors on a sunny window sill. As mentioned earlier, what you plant will be determined by what you like to eat, how you plan to store it, what crops you may be growing to sell or trade, and most importantly, what will grow well in your area of the country.

The important thing to remember in choosing your seed for the year 2000 is to buy NON-HYBRID, or open-pollinated, seed. Sometimes these are called "heirloom" varieties. Don't buy hybrid varieties. Hybrid seeds will grow beautiful crops, but if you gather their seeds and plant them next year, the resulting produce will be very inferior, and very possibly useless. Hybrid seeds don't "breed true". Non-hybrid seeds, however will produce the same results year after year. They are the kind you need if you're not able to buy new seed each spring. You must be able to gather your own garden seeds that can grow reliable crops.

NON-HYBRID SEED SOURCES

The following sources sell only non-hybrid varieties:

Butterbrooke Farm (203) 888-2000

G Seeds Star Route Box 73a, Oroville, WA 98844

Garden City Seeds (406) 961-4837

Gleckers Seedmen (419) 923-5463

Good Seed Co. Box 702, Tonasket, WA 98855 ($1 catalog)

J.L. Hudson Seedsmen Box 1058, Redwood City, CA 94064 ($1 catalog)

Native Seeds/Search 2509 N. Campbell,#325, Tucson, AZ85719

Redwood City Seed (415) 325-7333

Southern Exposure Seed Exchange Box 170, Earlysville, VA22936 ($2 for catalog)

Talavaya Seeds Box 707, Santa Cruz Station, NM 87507

($1 for catalog)

Vermont Bean Seed Co. (803) 663-0217

The Ark Institute

PO Box 142

Oxford, OH 45056

The following catalogs sell all kinds of seed: vegetables, flowers, hybrids and some non-hybrids. Hybrids are usually, but not always listed as such. Non-hybrids may be listed as "heirloom varieties".

Ferry Morse (800) 283-6400

Gurney's (605) 665-1930

Johnny's Selected Seeds (207) 437-4301

Pinetree Garden Seeds (207) 926-3400

R.H. Shumway's (803) 437-2733

The Cook's Garden (800) 457-9703

Some more common non-hybrid varieties (pumpkins, for example, and beans) will be for sale at the big chain discount stores like Wal-Mart or K-Mart at a good discount, but only in late winter and spring.

Recommended reading on gardening:

Order the following from Pinetree Garden Seeds 207- 926-3400:

Heirloom Vegetable Gardening, by William Woys Weaver

Rodale's All-New Encyclopedia of Organic Gardening, Bradley and Ellis

Garden Seed Inventory, by Kent Whealy

Gardening Under Cover, by William Head

Square-Foot Gardening, by Mel Bartholomew

Saving Seeds, by Marc Rogers

Seed to Seed, by Susan Ashworth

The following books are available from Ready-Made Resources 1-800--627-3809:

The Gardener's Bug Book, by Barbara Pleasant

Organic Gardener's Home Reference, by Tanya Denckla

The Mulch Book, by Stu Campbell

Four Season Harvest, by Eliot Coleman

Let it Rot, by Stu Campbell

The Delightful Delicious Daylily, by Peter Gail

Cold-Climate Gardening, by Lewis Hill

Backyard Composting, by Harmonius Technologies

The New Organic Grower, by Eliot Coleman

Step by Step Organic Vegetable Gardening, by Shepherd Ogden   Available from The Cook's Garden Catalog P.O. Box 535, Londonderry, VT 05148

SERIOUS FOOD PRODUCTION

People who are trying seriously to grow all their own food will need to grow some crops ordinary hobby gardeners usually don't: grains and dried beans.

192

GROWING GRAINS

Grains are one of the richest food sources on the planet for both man and beast.

RICE   Everyone is familiar with the concept of the rice paddy, and the type of rice grown there, the "lowland" type, is very productive. But there is another type that can be grown in drier areas, called the "upland" type. While still needing abundant rainfall, it can go as long as about three weeks without water, if necessary. Rice is most commonly grown in the Southern part of the U.S., but can be grown further north, providing you have a growing season of at least 40 days above 70 degrees.

CORN   There are many kinds of corn: sweet corn (the kind you eat fresh), popcorn, dent corn (the type primarily used as animal feed), flint corn (which is the most nutritious, stores very well and makes good cornmeal), and more. The important thing to remember is to buy non-hybrid varieties, whatever types you decide to grow.

Corn will grow in almost any soil, but it is what gardeners call a "heavy feeder": it really uses up the nutrients in the soil, so plan on enriching yours prior to planting with green or brown manure. Corn needs at least six hours a day of full sunlight, and does best where summers are hot.

WHEAT   Like corn, wheat does best in soil enriched with manure. Winter wheat is planted about the time of the first frost, grows through the winter, and is harvested when it has turned yellow in the spring or early summer. Spring wheat is planted about the time of the last frost, grows through the summer, and is ready to harvest when it has turned yellow in the fall. There are dozens of varieties and your best bet is to choose a variety grown in your area, but remember: choose a non-hybrid variety.

RYE   Rye grows well in poor soil and cool climates. It was a staple grain in Scandinavia. It is even hardier than wheat and the grain least susceptible to diseases and pests. It is also the easiest grain to thresh, though not as productive as some others. As with wheat, there are two planting times, winter or spring, but in the extreme northern parts of the U.S. and Canada, plant spring rye, as too much will die over the winter to make winter rye a good crop.

BARLEY has one problem: the husks cling tightly to the grain, making it hard to thresh unless you have a special mill for removing them. But it bears well, and early enough to plant with a hay crop which will grow on after the barley is harvested. Most livestock can eat barley whole, and it is possible to grind it whole for human consumption too, which will add plenty of fiber to the diet.

OATS do best in cool, moist climates like Scotland's, which is famous for its oats. A hull-less variety (Avena nuda) is available.

SORGHUM Like corn, sorghum needs nitrogen-rich soil, and can be grown anywhere you have at least 100 days above freezing. It can be grown in areas too hot and dry for corn. In the U.S. grain sorghum is primarily grown as livestock feed, but in other parts of the world people eat it too. Sweet sorghum can be grown for molasses or syrup production as well as for animal forage. Sorghum presses are available from Lehman's Non-electric Catalog.

AMARANTH Grain amaranths are the type that concern us here. They thrive in hot, dry climates, but need plenty of moisture after planting. They grow so luxuriantly weeds are not a problem, and they resist most insect pests too.

MILLET One of the most ancient human foods, millet is mainly grown in the U.S. now for birdseed. As a forage crop, millet can be fed as early as 30 days after sowing. It grows well in poor soil, stands up well to drought, and it good to plant on weedy land because it can outgrow the weeds.

QUINOA is native to the Andes, and does well in mountainous areas. It can't take extreme heat, but can withstand several degrees of frost.

BUCKWHEAT grows a very nutritious grain and is valuable to beekeepers as well. It is one of the best crops to grow on heavy clay soils, and one of the best to smother out weeds and grasses. It grows best in moist, cool parts of the country, but can be grown in other areas as well. If you live where it is hot and dry, consider planting mid-summer for a fall harvest. There are two types of buckwheat seed: the forage type and the grain type, so be sure you order what you want.

Because of possible crop failures, it is best to avoid growing just one grain. Sometimes the weather conditions or pests that wipe out one crop won't affect another, so diversify. Grow as many of these as your soil type and climate will allow. It is better nutritionally, too, to eat as large a variety of foods as possible, especially if you are on a vegetarian diet.

Grain-growing Resources:

Rodale Press' Small-Scale Grain Raising, by Gene Logsdon

Encyclopedia of Country Living by Carla Emery. In this essential book, Emery discusses raising, cutting, storing, threshing, grinding and cooking the various grains.

Lehman's Non-Electric Catalog, Box 41, Kidron, OH 44636, sells the various tools required for hand cutting, stacking, threshing and grinding grains. 330-857-5757

Seed Sources:

Abundant Life Seed Fdn. Box 772, Port Townsend, WA 98368 Catalog $2, newsletter for $20 membership

Bountiful Garden 18001 Shafer Ranch Rd. Willits, CA 95490

G Seeds Star Rt. Box 73A, Oroville, WA 98844

Seed Savers Exchange, 3076 N. Winn Rd. Decorah, IA 52101

Seeds of Change Boox 15700, Santa Fe, NM 87506

Lenz Schaller, KUSA, Box 761, Ojai, CA   93024

Peaceful Valley, Box 209, Grass Valley, CA 995945

Ronniger's, Star Rt. Road 73, Moyie Spgs, ID 83845 Catalog $1

Southern Exposure Seed Exchange, Box 158, North Garden, VA 22959

Catalog $2. They sell lowland and upland rice seed.

Polit Farms Box 625, Maxwell, CA 95955 Also sells rice seed.

Grain is heavy and shipping the quantities you'll need for self-sufficiency is expensive. If possible buy your grain seed from a local elevator or feed store; obtain from mail order only those varieties you can't get otherwise.

DRIED BEANS

Also called shell beans, these are easy to grow, and will do well even in poor soil. They thrive where it is hot but can be grown in cooler climates as well, because they have a short   growing season. They cannot, however, stand frost.

You can let them dry on the vine until they are mature and the beans are hard and dry, if you live in a dry enough locale. But if you live where it is rainy and humid, or you're expecting rain, you can pick the pods from the vines and dry under cover if necessary, or preferably outside in the sunshine. Spread out your beans in a single layer, wherever you spread them, and protect them from rain or dampness. Once dried, you shell them and store in a dry place. These are one thing you don't store in a root cellar. They store best in burlap bags or some other porous containers, but must be well protected from rodents.

There are thousands of varieties of beans, of all shapes and colors and sizes, but the main varieties are black, kidney, pinto, navy and pink beans.

Sources of Beans for seed:
Harris Seeds, 3670 Buffalo Rd., Rochester, NY 14624
Johnny's Selected Seeds, 229 Foss Hill Rd., Albion, ME 04910
Shumway, Box 4, Braniteville, SC 29829
Stokes Seed, Box 10, Catherines, Ontario, Canada L2R6R6 or Box 548,
Buffalo, NY 14240-0548
Twilley Seed Co. Box 65, Trevose, PA 19053
Vermont Bean Seed Co. Garden Lane, FairHaven, VT 005763

Novice farmers should unashamedly seek out advice from experienced old timers. Agricultural extension agents should be able to assist you with the spring and possibly fall 1999 season. Get in touch with them as early as you can to get all the advice they can give you.

AGRICULTURAL EXTENSION SERVICES
Alabama (205) 826-5323
Alaska (907) 277-1488
Arizona (602) 626-2438
Arkansas (501) 376-6301
California (916) 752-0412
             (209) 646-2794
             (714) 787-3432
Colorado (303) 491-7018
Connecticut (203) 486-3435
Delaware (302) 738-2531
             (302) 856-5250
District of Columbia (202) 282-7403
Florida (305) 475-8990
      (904) 392-2134
Georgia (404) 542-8861

Hawaii (808) 948-7256

Idaho (208) 334-3209

Illinois (217) 333-1969

Indiana (317) 749-2261

Iowa (712) 328-0077

Kansas (913) 532-6170

Kentucky (606) 257-2874

Louisiana (504) 388-4141

Maine (207) 581-2771

Maryland (301) 454-3143

Massachusetts (413) 545-2250

Minnesota (612) 376-7574

Mississippi (601) 325-3935

Missouri (314) 882-7511

Montana (406) 994-4601

Nebraska (402) 472-2454

Nevada (702) 784-6981

New Hampshire (603) 862-1200

New Jersey (201) 932-9393

New Mexico (505) 646-1521

New York, Cornell Univ. Ithaca, NY 14853

North Carolina (919) 737-3131

North Dakota (701) 237-8163

Ohio (216) 264-1021

Oklahoma, Okla. State Univ. Stillwater, OK 74078

Oregon (503) 754-3464

Pennsylvania (814) 863-2114

Puerto Rico (809) 832-4040, ex. 3004

Rhode Island (401) 792-2791

South Carolina (803) 656-3011

South Dakota (605) 688-5136

Tennessee (615) 974-7324

Texas (713) 845-7341

Utah (801) 750-2258

Vermont (802) 656-2630

Virgin Islands (809) 778-0246

Virginia (703) 961-6723

Washington (509) 335-2511

West Virginia (304) 293-4801

Wisconsin (608) 262-0768

Wyoming (307) 766-2243

APPENDIX H
WHAT ABOUT ANIMALS?

Every farm needs chickens. They are inexpensive, easy to raise, and the animal most likely to give you back as much as you put into it. Chickens don't need much room either, and could easily be raised in a small backyard, were it not for the fact that zoning regulations usually forbid it.

If it's eggs you're after, the single comb White Leghorn is probably the top white-egg producer. It is too small to be considered a meat bird, but this makes it an efficient egg producer, for it can lay as many eggs a year as a larger hen, but will eat much less feed. The New Hampshire, and Barred Plymouth Rock breeds are also good choices for egg production, though they will need more feed than the White Leghorn.

For meat, the Cornish and Cornish cross broilers will probably give you the most efficient feed-to-meat conversion ratios. By the time they're eight weeks old they will weigh in the seven-to-eight pound range, and be ready to butcher.

For an all-purpose chicken that will lay a good supply of eggs, but be worth eating too, try one of the "heavy breeds":   Rhode Island Red, Plymouth Rock, White Rock, Barred Rock, Wyandotte, and New Hampshire.

These modern, high-efficiency birds are great egg and meat producers, but the maternal instinct has been almost entirely bred out of them. They will give you eggs, but won't sit on the eggs and raise chicks.
To keep the hen-egg-chick cycle going, the trick is to keep a few bantam hens to sit on the eggs laid by your other hens. Bantam, or "Banty" hens are small, about one third the size of the larger breeds, and require little feed or space. The broodiest Bantam varieties are the Ancona, Brahma, Cochin, Faverolle and Silkies. They will mate with your larger breed rooster, and will sit on their own eggs, too, so you may end up with a number of them. Just be sure to eat the Bantam roosters, to prevent their less-productive bloodline from getting mixed in with your heavy-breed chickens.

HOW TO KEEP YOUR CHICKENS

Letting your chickens run or "range" free is best for them and for your land. Free-range chickens require much less feed than their penned counterparts, as they comb your property looking for insects and seeds to devour. They also freely fertilize your soil. They are less prone to diseases and cannibalization, too. But there are disadvantages: They will be a nuisance in your garden, and likely around your house, too. Dogs or hawks will probably make off with one occasionally, and you will have a merry Easter egg hunt every day trying to find their eggs.

But there is an arrangement which combines the advantages of penning with those of free-ranging: a movable pen, which is moved frequently to fresh grass.   Your bugs and ticks get eaten, ridding you of pests and reducing your feed bill, your soil gets fertilized, and your chickens (and their eggs) are safe from predators and where you want them. (And not where you don't want them!) If the chicken house has an open bottom, so much the better; it won't need much cleaning, and the droppings go where you want them; back to your soil. If you are raising meat birds, there is still another advantage: keeping them in a pen small enough to discourage much activity will give you much tenderer meat.

If you build your pen the normal way, stringing the fencing from posts, it is inconvenient to move, though it is possible. A better approach is to attach your fencing material to a frame, and put wheels on it. If the top is fenced too, your fowl will stay in better, be better protected from predators, and you can build the sides of the your pen shorter, maybe two feet high, saving you fencing material and weight. This movable pen approach is going to be more expensive than the typical stationary pen, and take longer to build, but will work much better.

Building one large pen would use less material than two small pens, but two smaller pens will give you more flexibility as well as convenience. Besides being easier to move, the smaller pens are better for raising meat birds, and having two pens is necessary for those times when you need to separate your flock; when new chicks hatch, for example, or when you bring in new birds and want to keep them separate from your flock for a few weeks.

WHERE DO I GET CHICKENS?

There are many options here, the easiest and probably cheapest is to order day-old chicks from your local feed store in the spring or summer, when most of them offer this service. You can also order them from the breeder yourself, which may cost a little more, but will give you more control over what breed you want and if you want pullets (young hens), cockerels (young roosters), or straight-run chicks (a random mix of both,

201

usually about half and half), as well as more choice of when to order and receive your chicks. Either way, they offer chicks only in batches of 25 and will only ship them when the weather is favorable to keeping baby chicks alive in a cardboard box.

Chick Hatcheries:

Inman Hatcheries, Box 616, Aberdeen, SD 57402, 605-225-8122

Bill Patterson, Rt. 9, Box 169, Martinsville, VA 24112 703-638-2297

Murray McMurray Hatchery (800) 456-3280

Stromberg's, HCR 77, Box 243, Pine River, MN 56474 218--587-2222

Your county extension agent or local 4H club can help you find a breeder or farmer near you who will sell you chicks, or even setting or laying hens. The latter would cost more, and may even be older, less-productive hens the farmer is secretly delighted to unload on a greenhorn like you, so if you choose this approach, be careful, unless you know the farmer.

Recommended reading on Poultry Raising:

Chicken Tractor by Andy Lee

Chickens in your Backyard by Rick and Gail Luttman

Raising Poultry Successfully by Will Graves

The Family Poultry Flock by Lee Schwartz

Also, Carla Emery's section on poultry raising in her very highly recommended Encyclopedia of Country Living has as much information as some complete books on the subject.

GOAT RAISING

In addition to a source of eggs you need a source of milk. Cows, sheep and goats are the most obvious choices to supply this demand, and our choice, as the animal most suited to the needs of a beginning farmer is the goat, for many reasons.

Cows give huge amounts of milk, as much as 12 gallons a day, and they are expensive, about $800-1,000 at this writing. Goats, on the other hand, produce at most, about a gallon of milk a day and cost about a hundred dollars. Their milk is better for humans than cow's milk, too, being easier to digest, and you can feed about five goats for what if would cost you to feed one cow. Goats, being much smaller, are also easier to handle, though they are harder to keep in their pen than a cow.

Although we have just been comparing goats and cows, they are really very different. Cows are grazers- they want to eat grass- and if you have a large grassy meadow, you should probably consider raising dairy or beef cattle or sheep. Goats are browsers, more like deer, they want to reach up, not down, for their food, and they eat the leaves of trees and shrubs. If you have a brushy hillside, or a plot overgrown with any kind of vines: brambles, poison ivy, kudzu, honeysuckle and the like, goats are your obvious choice. They will thrive on this fare, and clear your land for you while they're doing it.

The breed of goat is of little importance, if you are mainly thinking of milk production for your family, but you do want a dairy goat, not a fleece goat. The five most common milk breeds are: Alpine, La Mancha (the "earless" variety), Nubian, (the droopy-eared variety, reputed to be the most lovable), Saanen (the largest of these breeds), and Toggenburg. A cross of these breeds would likely cost you less, and give you as much milk as a purebred, though its kids would not fetch as high a price.

Another advantage to goats is that they are hardy and do not require fancy accomodations. A shelter from rain, wind and snow is enough. They can tolerate cold weather quite well in in unheated house if they have deep bedding, and the building is dry and draft-proof.

Goats are very social and sociable animals and you should never keep just one. To keep you in plenty of milk, you need one milking doe for each adult in your family. That will provide enough for your table, enough for their kids and probably some leftover for cheesemaking. Unless you are thinking of going in for goat breeding, or unless you live in a very remote area, far away from any other goat owners, you'd do better not buying a buck. A good start would be two or three does and their kids.

These organizations can help you find goat breeders in your area:
Alpines International, 557 S. Street,, Suffield, CT 06078
Internat'l .Nubian Breeder's Assn. Box 130, Creswell, OR 97426
National Saanen Breeders Assn. 8555 Sypes Cyn Rd. Bozeman, MT 59715
National Toggenburg Club, Box 531, Fort Collins, CO 80522

Also try your local 4H club and your extension agent. In addition, you may find goats for sale in the livestock section of your local newspaper.

Recommended reading about goats:
Raising Milkgoats the Modern Way by Jerry Belanger
Practical Goatkeeping by Jill and John Halliday
Raising Milkgoats Successfully by Gail Lutttmann

Goat Keepers' Supplies:
Caprine Supply, Box Y, DeSoto, KS 660018
Hoegger Supply Co. Box 331, Fayetteville, GA 30214

APPENDIX I
POWER CONSIDERATIONS

Advances are being made continually in alternative energy sources; solar, wind-driven, geothermal, and hydroelectric being the most usual. Mother Earth News magazine is one source of articles and books on these topics, and many others of interest to homesteaders. You can also get information from the library and over the internet, possibly even in the yellow pages in some areas of the country. You need to do some research to find out what will work best in your locale. If you live on the wind-swept Great Plains, for example, windmills and solar applications are good bets; if you live near a year-round swiftly-flowing stream, you should look into hydroelectric power. Geothermal can work nearly anywhere, but would provide only heat, not energy for other appliances or lighting.

BOOKS ON SOLAR, HYDROELECTRIC and WIND ENERGY
Available from Ready-Made Resources 1-800-627-3809:

MicroHydro Power
Our Own Solar Energy Catalog
Wind Power for Home and Business, by Paul Gipe
The Real Goods Solar Living Sourcebook
Fuel From Water, by Michael A. Peavey

Check with local dealers for advice about the best equipment for your area:

Alternative Energy Engineering, Inc.
Business type: distributor
Product types: batteries, PV modules, small wind-powered electric generators, hydro powered electric generators.
Address: P.O. Box 339, Redway, CA USA 95560
Telephone: (800) 777-6609
Web Site: http://www.alt-energy.com
E-mail: energy@alt-energy.com

Alternative Energy Systems Co. of Mississippi
Business type: distributor, service
Product types: solar panels, wind & hydro generators, systems.
Address: 22 Dillard Road, Poplarville, MS USA 39470
Telephone: 601-772-9966
Web Site: http://members.aol.com/aescoms/aes.htm
E-mail: aescoms@aol.com

Bay Winds
Business type: distributor
Product types: Midwest Jacobs Wind Energy Dealer, small wind-powered generators (10 to 20 kW).
Address: 1533 Kimball Street, Green Bay, WI USA 54302
Web Site: http://www.baywinds.com
E-mail: sales@baywinds.com

CI Solar Supplies Co
Business type: manufacturer, distributor
Product types: PV Modules, Components, Solar Water Heaters, Wind Electric Generators,
Address: 12715 Wright Ave, Chino, CA USA 91710
Telephone: (909) 628-6440
FAX: (909) 628-6440
Web Site: http://www.cisolar.com/cisolar.htm
E-mail: jclothi@ibm.net

Electron Connection
Business type: distributor
Product types: batteries, hydro-powered generators, DC to AC inverters, PV modules, solar cooking products, water pumps, wind-powered generators.

Service types: mail-order, site survey, design and installation
Address: P.O. Box 203, Hornbrook, CA USA 96044
Telephone: (800) 945-7587
FAX: (916) 475-3401

Energy Outfitters Ltd.
Business type: distributor
Product types: PV Modules, DC to AC inverters, small wind-powered electric generators,
hydro-powered electricgenerators.
Service types: system design
Address: 136 S. Redwood Hwy., Cave Junction, OR USA 97523
Telephone: (541) 592-6903
FAX: (541) 592-6747
Web Site: http://www.energyoutfitters.com
E-mail: sales@energyoutfitters.com

Fran-Mar Alternative Energy
Business type: distributor, service
Product types: hydro-powered generators, microhydro-powered generators, PV modules, wind-powered generators.
Service types: system design, consultation, installation
Address: Box 163E Babcock Road, Camden, NY USA 13316
Telephone: 315.245.3916

Go Solar
Business type: distributor, service
Product types: PV modules Wind Generators Hot water heaters Pool heaters Charge controllers.
Address: 1446 Flanders Road, Riverhead, NY USA 11901
Telephone: 516-727-2224
Web Site: http://www.hamptons.com/gosolar
E-mail: gosolar@hamptons.com

Kansas Wind Power
Business type: distributor
Product types: DC to AC inverters, solar related products, water pumps, wind-powered generators.
Address: Route 1, Holton, KS USA 66436
Telephone: (913) 364-4407

Lake Michigan Wind & Sun

Business type: distributor
Product types: PV modules, wind-powered generators.
Service types: sales, service and installation
Address: 1015 County Rd U, Sturgeon Bay, WI USA 54235
Telephone: 920/ 743-0456
E-mail: lmwands@itol.com

Mid South Alternate Energy
Business type: distributor, service
Product types: PV modules, wind-powered electric generators,
hydro-powered electric generators.
Address: 6530 Finch Rd, Memphis, TN USA 38141
Telephone: 901-362-8944
E-mail: bobjones@desotoonline.com

Offshore Services, Ltd
Business type: distributor, service
Product types: Design, Install, Maintain Renewable Energy
windpowered generators.
Service types: design and installation
Address: 100 Ocean Ave, Block Island, RI USA 02807
Telephone: (401) 466-2875
E-mail: offshore@wind-power.com

Sierra Solar Systems
Business type: distributor
Product types: PV modules, Books and Publications, small
wind-powered electric generators.
Address: 109 Argall Way, Nevada City, CA USA 95959
Telephone: (916) 265-8441
Web Site: http://www.sierrasolar.com
E-mail: solarjon@oro.net

Solar Plexus
Business type: distributor
Product types: microhydro-powered generators, PV modules,
wind-powered generators.
Address: 130 West Front Street, Missoula, MT USA 59802
Telephone: 406-721-1130
Web Site: http://www.marsweb.com/solplex
E-mail: solplex@marsweb.com

Susitna Energy Systems
>   Business type: distributor
>   Product types: PV, wind generators, hydro generators, energy
>   Toyo oil stoves.
>   Address: 8230 EAST 19TH, Anchorage, AK USA 99504
>   Telephone: 907-337-1300
>   E-mail: kirkg@alaska.net

Tri Wind Solar Energy Systems And Products
>   Business type: distributor
>   Product types: solar products, wind-powered generators.
>   Address: 22402 Piessner Rd Se, Yelm, WA USA 98597
>   Telephone: 360-894-3675

Wind Solar and Water Systems
>   Business type: manufacturer, distributor, service
>   Product types: wind-powered generators, small
>   wind-powered
>   Address: 2101 North Fourth St Suite 220,
>   Flagstaff, AZ 86004
>   Telephone: 520-774-6341
>   Web Site: http://www.wswsystems.com
>   E-mail: info@wswsystems.com

Windstream Power Systems Inc.
>   Business type: manufacturer, distributor
>   wind-powered generators.
>   Address: One Mill Street P.O. Box 1604-HP,
>   Burlington, VT 05402-1604
>   Telephone: (802) 658-0075
>   FAX: (802) 658-1098
>   E-mail: windstrm@ix.netcom.com

LIGHTING

No matter what your fuel or energy plans, you need backup lighting. It can be a generous store of candles or old-fashioned kerosene lanterns and a good supply of kerosene.

Good sources for kerosene lanterns of every description, parts for them, replacement chimneys and many, many other items invaluable for non-electric living are the Lehman's Non-Electric catalog, the Cumberland General Store Catalog and Ready-Made Resources 1--800-6277-3809

GENERATORS: Keep in mind that even with generated electricity, not all appliances will work. Anything especially high-tech or computer-controlled could have trouble unless you have an electrician carefully calibrate the output of the generator and the interface to your home wiring. Macintosh computers or some of the later PCs should, in theory, work. Simple items like pumps for wells, or hot plates won't have any problems. Late model refrigerators or freezers may not work.

If all you want generated power for is refrigeration, then think about a kerosene powered freezer from Lehman Non Electric (330 857 5757).

If you need generated power for other reasons, you can buy an 8kw CDI diesel fuel generator for about $3000. It will last 50,000 hours (about five years, or about 17 years if you run it only 8 hours a day) and burn about 12,500 gallons before it needs an overhaul. They give you repair kits when you buy it that gets you another 50,000 hours. You can contact the manufacturer at 619-669-1995.

Inverters to get the power into your house can be bought from Kansas Wind Power, 13569 214th Rd., Holton, KS 66434.

APPENDIX J

The Church as Primary Neighbor

In the U.S. today, most families are living such selfish and busy lives that relationships with neighbors are shallow at best, and unfriendly at worst.

In time of crisis neighbors can sometimes mean the difference between life and death, or easy and hard living. If relationships with neighbors can be strengthened before the crisis, it can be possible to come to understandings about division of labor and responsibility that can make everyone's lives easier.

For example, if Joe the golfer has a big yard that's suitable for growing wheat, and Sam the construction worker has a yard that won't grow wheat but will grow potatoes, they can decide ahead of time what to plant, and share the results. If Jack the policeman can't grow anything on his land, maybe Jack can help Joe and Sam look after their crops and share accordingly.

The bigger your network of cooperative neighbors, the better your standard of living can be. Before you try to organize existing groups of people, like the neighborhood swimming pool membership, give some thought to the likely results of your efforts. Some groups, like some homeowners' associations, may have more built in animosity toward members than good will. Some groups, like the local BFOPFWCCG (Brotherhood of The Fraternal Order of Proud Fellows Who Like Closed, Comfortable Groups with Rules and Ceremonies that Remind All Members That They're Officially Part of a Closed Comfortable Group) may not be too open to be neighborly with a new group of neighbors.

It is important to take an active role in organizing your neighbors because undesirable groups will form if the law abiding majority is not forming its own groups of neighbors. Gangs and organized crime cartels can flourish where there is a vacuum of organized leadership. After the so-called fall of the Soviet Union, the Russian Mafia seized a choke hold on neighborhoods and neighborliness that reached into other nations. According to scholars at Georgetown University, the Russian mob has been able to extend its control of business and government into 38 of the 50 United States. The reasons given by these scholars is a vacuum of local leadership, or a presence of corrupt leadership.

The groups that are the most likely to lead the community out of chaos are the churches, primarily because of a basic traditional structure that keeps pastors from being petty tyrants and encourages all members to be servants of each other in doing deeds of benevolence with a spirit of teamwork. This same church structure is often dynamic enough to permit newcomers to bring in ideas and energy that can be plugged in to the expansion of doing good to the community.

Of course, there are local churches that are unproductive nightmares of unChristian bureaucracy, and you may have had a distasteful experience with a church like this that has kept you away from church for 30 years. You may consider yourself an agnostic. You may consider yourself too worldly to be welcome in any church. Check out your local churches anyway, especially the smaller ones. You might be surprised at what you find. Some churches have already taken admirable steps to care for the weaker members of the congregation and also for hundreds of others in the community, including refugees that might travel into the community. One church just acquired several hundred acres of land that can be farmed by unemployed members of the congregation. Another church just purchased two semi-truck-loads of MRE's, the military meals that have a long shelf life.

Throughout modern history, the powerful continuity of church structure has been a remarkable social fixture. Even weak churches are strong institutions in times of crisis. One of the best examples of this paradox is the German church of the mid-20th Century. In the 1930s, the Protestant church was as weak and double-minded as today's American Protestant church. Pastors and congregants were worried about what the world thought of them, and compromise with the world was a part of church mentality. Less than one percent of pastors were willing and courageous enough to resist the anti-Christian Furher, who came to despise these weak pastors for their cowardice. To gain approval from the state, some pastors even joined the SS and pledged loyalty to Hitler. Naziism was clearly a non-Christian ideology, but many churches displayed swastika banners that were draped over balcony railings in the sanctuaries.

Hitler gloated contemptuously, "Do you really believe the masses will be Christian again? Nonsense! Never again. That tale is finished. No one will listen to it again. But we can hasten matters. The parsons will dig their own graves. They will betray their God to us. They will betray anything for the sake of their miserable jobs and salaries."

By the time Hitler and the Third Reich were defeated, many pastors who had vouched for Hitler's good intentions had been routinely executed. But the churches were still there. The structure was still there. The memberships of many churches were smaller, but they were still there. Every government institution was gone. Every government service was gone. Every soldier, every bureaucrat, every policeman of the Third Reich was gone from any official function. But the institution of the church stood. As refugees from East Germany poured into West, as the nation tried to rebuild from nothing, the churches were the active instruments of health, education, welfare, charity and local leadership.

When US municipal governments fall after January, 2000, and after the federal government vanishes like a vapor, it will be the churches that can stand as stable institutions to hold together the fabric of society. Of course the churches will only be as strong as their congregations, but communities will begin to look even to weak churches for guidance, help and direction.

If you relocate to the country, you should get into a decent church even if it's not organized for y2k. You may be able to help it get organized. If you do, then in the year 2000, you may find your family surrounded by dozens of other very grateful families who become a great help to you.

The following "Open letter to Pastors" was written to try to educate pastors who don't see the dangers of y2k. Feel free to copy this letter and send it out.

The State of the Church
in the last months of the twentieth century

An open letter to Christian pastors
on the dangers of year 2000 computer failure
and how the Church can be a blessing to others
during a period of significant
uncertainty, hardship, and need.

Sirs:

Since the 1970's, computer people have been speculating about the "millennium bug," or the "Y2K (year two thousand) bug." These are names for the computer problems that will appear at midnight, December 31, 1999, when some mainfame computer programs and some computer chips will begin to malfunction because they are not prepared to deal with the date rollover to January 1, '00. This simple, two digit problem seems easy enough to overcome, and as late as the early 1990s scientists and engineers fully expected to see a solution to this simple problem.

But it is now 1997 and no easy solution has appeared. Many programmers are working feverishly to repair inadequate date codes, but they are admitting that the repair process began too late[1] , and that many critical systems will

not be ready for the deadline.[2]   This is not because the problem is difficult

to fix. It is because the problem is contained in billions of lines of

computer codes -- long, complicated lines -- that must be corrected by hand.

Line by line, digit by digit.[3] As these programmers project how their

[1] Congressman Stephen Horn of the House subcommittee on Government Management, Information, and Technology, is furious that business leaders and government agencies have not moved responsibly to address the problem and to move toward adequate repair. His April and September 1996 hearings document a record of failure and irresponsibility. Senator D'Amato says bluntly that this is a catastrophe "which could endanger the financial well-being of hundreds of millions of Americans." Congressman John Dingell referred to "the catastrophic business and economic consequences" of the millennium bug, and a memorandum from the Library of Congress's Congressional Research Service (CRS) has warned that "it may be too late to correct all of the nation's systems."

[2] The most candid discussions among programmers and project managers can be found in the internet discussion forum organized by Peter de Jager at amy@year2000.com. For more than two years these programmers have put their heads together to find y2k solutions, and have admitted their failures very openly. These are programmers from all over the world, and the consensus, recorded in thousands of pages, is that the deadline will not be reached.

[3] According to CIO Magazine September 15, 1996 issue, an article appeared, "Will Your Systems Survive the Year 2000?" It reported on Social Security: "By June 1996, changes were complete for six million lines of code, with 24 million left to go" (p. 58) , The Social Security Administration has corrected only six million lines of code in five years, and must complete another 24 million lines of code in a little over a year.They have not yet completed inventory of operating systems, which keep the overall system running. Citicorp has a staggering total of 400 million lines of code to check. Citicorp began its fix in 1995 (Investor's Business Daily, Feb. 12, 1997.). Its noncompliant code may be larger than Social Security's entire system. Chase Manhattan has 200 million lines of code (Software Magazine, March 1997, p. 32) . As for the Federal Reserve System, our nation's central bank, it is in the assessment stage (Federal Reserve Bank of Atlanta, Financial Update, Oct.-Dec. 1996, p. 3)of the process, and has not begun the repair operation.

failing systems can affect other systems[4], and realize just how computer-dependent Western society has become[5] , their admissions and predictions are taking a serious tone[6] that should alarm all of us. The following letter was not written with alarmist terms or motives, but is offered as a friendly "heads-up" to leaders who wish to understand the times so that they may display strength and take action.

A simple summary of the times (related to this computer problem) can be stated this way:

> Y2K is a simple problem to fix, but no major
> company, bank or government agency has yet
> succeeded. No government agency or utility
> anywhere in the world that can claim that their
> computers or software will operate properly on
> January 1, 2000. If major systems fail, results could
> be disastrous.[7] The results can theoretically be *so*
> disastrous that many political people and some

---

[4] Correcting and repairing the code is time consuming because of the sheer magnitude of the task, and because each correction must be tested to see if the "fix" causes problems elsewhere in the program.

[5] Computers have been tasked to run virtually every aspect of employment, banking, transportation, food supply and utilities in functions that touch our lives every hour on the hour.

[6] *You Can't Overestimate Y2K's Effect*, Chicago Tribune, December 29, 1997. Veteran programmer George Hawkins, 66, says it will affect every life on a daily basis, creating havoc. Hawkins has emerged from retirement to try to help. "Many people will be forced to leave jobs very quickly," says Hawkins.

[7] *Is Y2K Real or Surreal?*, December 8, 1997, amcity.com/twincities/stories

technical people are simply denying[8] that the
computers could fail, even though they have no
evidence to support their denial.[9]

How many computers are likely to fail?

It's not the number of failures that matters. The question should be, "which
computers will fail, and will those failures hurt us?" At the time of this
writing, some of the most important mainframe computer programs will
not be ready - programs that run important functions like banking
transactions, railroad schedules, and electrical power stations. Even if only a
few of these mainframes crash, those few failures can compromise hundreds
of other systems within hours.

**What will Year 2000 computer failure mean for the average
American family?**

Some home PC's will fail, but this small problem will not threaten society
or family safety. The problem lies with mainframe computer programs that

---

[8] *Waiting for Millenium Panic Level to Rise,* New York Times, January 5,
1998. Cap Gemini's survey of 109 technology firms found that four out of
five had underestimated the problem. "A lot of companies, when they found
out how big the problem was, just went into a catatonic state," reports Jim
Woodward.

[9] Most assertions that equipment and software will work are based on
wishful thinking rather than hard test evidence. As of January, 1998 there is
no known hardware test that has worked without a flaw. Most software tests
cannot even be run until more code repair is accomplished. Most companies
and government agencies are in the "assesment" stage of the process.
After this stage comes years of repair and testing and retesting. American
Management Systems has reported, "Even if all Year 2000 snafus are fixed,
the resulting format inconsistencies will create 1,768 ambiguous dates that
computers could misinterpret in the first decade of the new millennium."

now control the essential business of Western civilization. Because every family has come to depend on mainframe computer programs, it means that some families could be facing periods of days or months or years without money, banking services, running water, electricity, stocked grocery shelves, reliable automobiles, household heat, telephone service, refrigeration, or government services like mail delivery and police protection.

What will this mean for society?
Each of the services and conveniences listed above depend on mainframe computers or embedded computer chips. As of June, 1997 every one of these conveniences are threatened with some predictable failures or disruptions.[10] These potential failures have been documented, and warnings for each have been issued in writing. Other predictable failures are deliberately being covered up on the advice of legal counsel. Because some corporations are deliberately keeping Americans in the dark, no one will know for sure how bad things could be until Monday morning, January 3, 2000.

If the disruptions last only a matter of days, society will survive just fine. People will face unprecedented levels of aggravation, frustrating levels of

---

[10] The greatest collection of predicted failures is contained in the files of the **Damocles Project**, which is organizing files for litigation discovery processes. Damocles can be contacted at year2000.com. The latest estimated cost of lawsuits in the US alone is $1.3 Trillion. Securities class action attorneys are leaping on the y2k problem as a potential gold mine. According to the New York Times, January 1, 1998, "that...is the best indicator yet of the size of the problem that looms."

inconvenience, but then life will go on[11]. People will look back on the year 2000 problem as a nuisance and a technological "hiccup."

But, if any single disruption lasts more than two weeks, it will have a domino-like effect on other strained services and institutions of society. The dangers[12] of the domino effect can create a scenario in which <u>sudden, massive unemployment, the explosive spread of disease and crime, political anarchy, government collapse and wholesale despair</u> could weigh heavily on every developed country for six to ten years[13] .

Is such a grave scenario possible? Yes. Credible experts[14] are now

---

[11] For most folks, that is. According to the London Sunday Times, December 11, 1997, even a three day computer flaw "could kill patients" in average hospitals because of failures in equipment. See also techweb.com, and Computerweekly, December 11, 1997.

[12] *The Domino Effect,* Inc. Magazine, December 1, 1997. Reports computer expert, "We're all of us done in by the domino effect."

[13] *Millennium Timebomb: An American Nightmare,* The Guardian, January 16, 1998. See also *Millennium Problem Affects Linked Global Economy,* Computerworld, February 2, 1998. See aslo Edward Yourdon's new book *Time Bomb 2000,* in which he writes, "...we think athat a very small percentage of y2k problems could be sufficiently devastating that it could could take a decade to recover. "

[14] *A List of Major Dominoes,* The Institute of Electrical Engineers, November 4, 1997. See also *2000 Threat Real, Experts Say,* Wichita Eagle, January 16, 1998, and *U.S. Not Ready For Y2K,* Reuters, January 1, 1998.

predicting widespread disruptions, including a bank collapse[15] that will

demolish the present economies[16] in North America, Japan and Europe[17].

One of the more serious calculations[18] was just released by Rick Cowles,

power grid expert, who has discovered that electrical power outages[19] in the

[15] *Banks Face Concerns over Y2K Problem,* Houston Business Journal, January 5, 1998. *For Banks, Time is Up for Y2K,* Baltimore Business Journal, January 5, 1998. *Will Your Bank Live to See The Millennium?* Business Week, January 26, 1998. Also see Forbes Magazine, July 28, 1997, and the Senate Banking Committee web site at senate.gov/`banking/index.htm. The Federal Reserve calls the risks "substantial" and worries that 70% of banks are not even addressing the fact that their software programs need to be converted - rewritten to recognize dates in the 21st century. "This lack of planning could result in the extended or permanent disruption of computer system operations.... This issue affects EVERY financial institution...." The Wall Street Journal concludes that "The looming "year 2000" software conversion issue brings a chill to those who realize its seriousness...A failure to complete this conversion "would mean a major disabling..., and then they describe the failure of the most critical government agency - which is the agency that ultimately funds every government service from military, to mail delivery to air traffic control - the IRS. Former IRS historian Shelley Davis believes the IRS computer system repair process is hopeless.

[16] *A Race Against The Calendar,* December 7, 1997, New York Times. Ed Yardeni, chief economist at Deutche Morgan Grenfell, predicts a year-long global recession. See also U.S. Senate Banking, Housing and Urban Affairs Committee, November 4, 1997 hearings at which Yardeni was an expert witness. senate.gov/`banking/97_11hrg/

[17] *Canadian Bank Official Warns of World Economic Crisis,* Computer World, January 14, 1998. Joe Boivin leaves his post at the CIBC to create the National Millennium Foundation in Ottawa.

[18] Cowles is considered the leading authority on electric utilities. According to Cowles (euy2k.com), "Based on what I learned at DistribuTECH '98, I am convinced that there is a 100% chance that a major portion of the domestic electrical infrastructure will be lost as a result of the Year 2000 computer and embedded systems problem. The industry is fiddling while the infrastructure burns."

[19] December 16, 1997 London Sunday Times, *Utilities Face Threat of y2k Penalty*

US may be total, and that outages in some areas may last longer than six months, with some repairs requiring years.

Under such conditions society as we know it will not survive.[20]
Because such a thought is "unthinkable," lots of otherwise responsible people are refusing to think about the logical results and consequences of potential[21] realities. Reality is being ignored or denied.

How will pastors respond?

It is my prayer that pastors will act like men, and will not go along with the present worldly denial that "things can't possibly be that bad, and besides, Bill Gates or some other genius will come up with a silver bullet to fix y2k.[22] " One pastor told me he couldn't allow himself to think about what could happen because his congregants would not allow themselves to think such dreadful thoughts. Another told me he wants nothing to do with fear and would not say anything that would cause his people to be afraid.

It is not fear-mongering to see danger and then to practice and preach caution. It is the fool who plunges ahead with misplaced confidence.[23]   I

[20] Western man is dependent not only on modern conveniences, but on a free market that keeps supplies at our fingertips, and on a debt structure that permits us to live paycheck-to-paycheck without an emergency cushion of two-to-three years' savings for times of hardship. In the words of one economist, modern society is dependent on three institutions, all of which are threatened if y2k disruptions last longer than two months: The fractional reserve banking system, electricity, and government schooling. If even two of these three go down, society will require re-tooling from the local level up. It is not government's job to create culture and society.

[21] *Y2k Already Taking Its Toll,* Infoworld, January 10, 1998.

[22] *Too Late For Silver Bullet,* Computer World, January 26, 1998.

[23] Proverbs 22:3

believe pastors must face the reality that society as we know it could cease
to exist. But is this calamity or opportunity? A curse or a blessing?
Doom and gloom or occasion for spiritual triumph? Will the Church of
Jesus Christ be discredited or will it prosper? If people are not ready to face
the potential hardships and turn the situation to the Lord's advantage, it will
be a scary time with real physical dangers. But if people are ready, the Y2k
problem is not to be feared, but welcomed.

For godly Christian leaders, the y2k crisis is a wonderful opportunity, and it
is in this spirit of Biblical optimism that this letter is written. It is an
opportunity for leaders to act decisively. To prevent anarchy, promote
civilized conduct, and to rise to their full calling, Christian leaders have an
unprecedented opportunity to minister, serve, lead, inspire, make disciples
and rebuild. If they and their congregations are ready for the year 2000 crisis,
the Church will be a shining example of Christlike maturity. If the Church
is not ready, her members and leaders may be overcome by panic, and
behave as shamefully as other members of society with whom they are
completing for scarce resources.

How will the Church respond?

The Church will follow the lead of her leaders. Mainframe computer failures
in just three government agencies could mean that soldiers, policemen,
mailmen, judges, and tax collectors may go without paychecks for an
indefinite period. If they leave their posts, our society could devolve to a
nineteenth century framework in which local government bears the burden of
governing. Students of history know this is how it should be, and how our
Founders designed it, but a sudden return to a more proper civil order will
not be an orderly event.

But we should welcome that event as a long-term improvement. Federal Reserve, IRS, Social Security and military computer systems[24] might be so feeble that today's vastly bloated, unconstitutional government could undergo a turbulent collapse. The collapse could be so rapid, dictatorial alternatives[25] may be entirely unworkable. Virtually all federal government controls could fade away and the American people could find themselves face-to-face with many of the same challenges of self-government and local government that America's founders addressed[26] . This would be good, not bad.

But if local police and magistrates are AWOL or overburdened, the community will lean on, or hide from, whatever leaders emerge. Our current godless culture could readily produce leaders that run the the community through local organized crime cartels. Indeed, crime bosses took over the civil order as the Soviet Union collapsed, and the Russian mob has now extended its affairs into 38 of the 50 United States. They succeed in the US because there is a vacuum of leadership. It's time for the American Church to aggressively rise to the occasion and exercise its corporate calling and duty. It's time for Church leaders to emerge as community leaders. It must

---

[24] *Pentagon Shooting Blanks At Y2k, Entire Government Faces Problem,* Denver Post, January 28, 1998.

[25] Some analysts fear that minor disruptions would provide an excuse for power-hungry bureaucrats to use agency powers, executive orders and other extra-constitutional means to assume greater authoritarian controls than any government ever wielded. Banking and employment emergencies would indeed provide this opportunity. But the disruptions could out-pace the usurpations, and there simply may not be enough government agents to make a new form of tyranny possible. See Chicago Tribune, December 1, 1997, *Retired Troops Available for y2k Emergency.*

[26] *Millennium Bug Could Cripple Government,* BBC News, January 15, 1998.

happen now, before the computer crisis is overwhelming.[27]

In the days of our founders, the clergy were the most respected leaders, teachers and governors of society. Pastors did not shrink from speaking and acting on the tough issues of the day because they had a confidence that God's word contained applicable wisdom for those issues.

The Church is fully equipped and charged to be the first instrument of community education, health, charity, public conscience and welfare. This does not mean that America ever was or should be an ecclesiocracy (a nation run by the clergy of an official state Church), but we should remember that America's first and best public servants were men of the Church - they were Church leaders who acted as individual public servants.[28]

---

[27] The very nature of this crisis requires that action be taken ahead of time. Preparation will be necessary to forestall situations of unmanageable confusion.

[28] America's Founders had a remarkably Biblical perspective on the respective roles of Church and State. Cotton Mather spoke for most when he described Church and State as separate institutions and separate authorities that worked in parallel. Both were to function under the precepts of Biblical law, and neither was to have authority over the other. It was never confusing or conflicting for Christian men to serve in either institution, or both simultaneously. During the y2k crisis, it may be necessary for most Christian leaders to serve in both simultaneously. It may also be necessary for Christian men to serve the civil government by aggressively reorganizing, rebuilding and redefining the duties of the local civil government. This task will not be as daunting as it appears, because the only two legitimate functions of local civil government are the administration of justice and the pysical protection of the citizenry. If Christian public servants kept the roles of Church and State in Biblical perspective, this would provide additional support needed for the Church to reclaim her rightful position as the primary caretaker of health, education and welfare.

Is Godly Public Service a Lost Ministry?

In this letter I am pleading with today's pastors, elders, deacons and churchgoing fathers to prepare themselves to become visible and masculine public servants in the coming public distress. This does not mean they should campaign for elective office, but it does mean they must be ready to assume responsibilities of civic office or civic duty on short notice. It means they must make their churches stronger than they have ever been. It means they must give thought to what "tough times" will do to their families, their churches and their immediate communities. They must prepare themselves to rise up in the crisis to publicly point the way to the other side of the crisis. It means they should give thought to what it means to serve others in the tradition of the Lord Jesus -- as shepherd, protector, guide and friend of strangers.

The crisis won't last a lifetime, but it will last long enough for the Church to discover great opportunities in the misfortunes of the y2k turmoil. If today's leaders would prepare their congregations for the specific hardships that may fall on the nation, the Church can assume its cultural mandate again, and again wear a mantle of respectability. It goes without saying that the top priority in this mandate is the ministry of reconciliation of men to God through Jesus Christ and the power of the gospel message. According to historian and economist Gary North, the crisis may be the greatest opportunity for evangelism in world history.

However, the following suggestions for community ministry will be brief and limited to ways the Church can stand far above the crisis as salt and light, ministering nobly to the bodily needs of individuals and families, and ministering wisely to the very real civil needs of a community in need of

Biblical shepherding.

What should Pastors do?

Prepare their people for the work of service. The main obstacle to community Church action is that Christians are not used to doing much more than distributing unwanted clothing or canned goods to small local charities. When it comes to upholding justice, standing up to community enemies, defending the rights of the poor and defenseless, distributing scarce food supplies to truly hungry people, calming civil unrest, we're downright inexperienced. We don't know what it means to "stand in the gates."

There's no time to argue about why Christians abandoned the political and public policy spheres and retreated into Christian ghettos. The issue at hand is that Christians must strengthen one another with the courage to venture out - to venture back into the arenas of civil government, and church-organized health, education and welfare programs.

A good place to start is to realize that it's perfectly fine for men of the Church to be involved in the affairs of the community -- legal affairs, legislative affairs, law enforcement affairs, judicial affairs, civil defense affairs, water and sewer affairs, political affairs and anything else that affects the families of the community.

The next thing to do is begin to discuss the specifics of the y2k threat with trusted Church members. Pastors must realize that if the crisis is severe and their Churches are not ready, their members will probably behave as shamefully as starving survivalists who serve themselves first, and who see all neighbors as competitors for limited food[29] and water supplies.

This shame will be an unnecessary reproach to the body of Christ. Hunger and poverty drives men with weak character to disgraceful extremes. Pastors must strengthen the character of their flocks, must inform them about possible hardships, and then lead a preparation effort that divides labor and responsibility throughout the congregation, so that problems of hunger and poverty are lessened and so that individual members can bear the burdens of those in the Church, and extend charity and hospitality to those outside.

If the pastor can strengthen his relationship with other clergymen, he can help divide community responsibilities among churches.

The U.S. is the most computer-dependent nation on earth, and its people are arguably the most spoiled and unprepared for hardship of any people in history. No one knows what will happen to the civil order if the crisis is severe and if recovery takes more than five years.[30] Truly, the character of the American people is weak, undisciplined and depraved. Their knowledge of small-scale agriculture is limited. The national food supply is smaller than it has been for decades. If middle-class baby-boomers lose the value of their mutual funds in a market crash brought on by a computer crisis that wipes out even 30% of American jobs, the country could face greatly exaggerated chaotic conditions.

---

[29] Several factors have contributed to a current food shortage that is worse than it has been in the US for many decades. Famine could touch modern America. See *Danger in Food Supply*, US News &World Report, November 24, 1997; and the several dozen excellent archived food supply updates at arkinstitute.com/97/30nov97.htm

[30] *Countdown to a Digital Disaster*, London Sunday Times, December 12, 1997.

A panic-stricken populace might beg the government to assume dictatorial powers. Power-hungry politicians may abuse their duties "in the name of the people" regardless of what the people want.

However, if Church leaders are standing in the gap before a general panic, then the Church can rise to a position of ministry and service that would bring great glory to the precepts on which the Church of Jesus Christ is founded.

Large cities will be hardest hit[31], and pastors of big city congregations would be well advised to urge their members to plan escape routes to rural areas where they may be able to live for extended periods with friends or relatives. Logistics for managing the crisis in the cities should include only those men and resources that will stay in the city.

Rural Church congregations may wish to issue invitations to urban congregants. In suburban and rural Churches, the nature of the crisis calls for entire communities to be entirely self sufficient. Pastors should know how a community would fare if cut off from outside supplies of electricity, water, food and medical supplies.

What are the alternative sources? How many generators would it take to pump a minimum of fresh water? How much fuel would be needed to operate the generators? Which wells will be safest? How and where could food be stored? How much should be bought now, and who will pay for it?

---

[31] *New York City Will Be Like Beirut,* Computer Weekly, November 19, 1997. "First level managers know their projects [are] doomed, but they can't talk publicly about it," says y2K expert Ed Yourdon.

If U.S. currency goes out of circulation, what alternative forms of currencies or scrip could a community adopt? What agricultural pursuits can be delegated to unemployed fathers so that sufficient varieties of crops are being produced? What land can be made available for wise use of community labor? In what ways can local farmers be recruited to serve as leaders of the agricultural projects? What should be the policies of food distribution outside the community if others are starving? How can the community be set up to handle refugees from areas that are worse off?[32]

This is a challenge of real leadership. It will take clarity of vision to see the scope and nature of the problem, and great patience to explain it even in the face of ridicule. It will take uncommon wisdom to persuade today's dream-world Christians that the problems could be severe. It will take uncommon courage to attack the problems consistently without discouragement. It will take work to organize the logistics. It will take persistence to keep on track. If the situation is severe, the tough decisions will be gut wrenching experiences, especially those about food distribution. If your community is hungry, but the nearby big city is starving, and there is a truck that could

---

[32] Answers to many of these logistical questions can be found in The "Forum" Section of www.remnant.org. Some Christians are forming y2k communities established for the purpose of communal strength, medium scale agriculture, and family security. In these small, planned communities, houses are arranged for community protection, power is derived from solar or hydro electric plants on the property, and the land is divided into arable sections farmed by each family in a capitalistic, rather than communistic, arrangement. For families who do not have the means to move to the safety of one of these communities, local churches must offer, at the very least, information about similar levels of security and opportunity for small scale agricultural pursuits within the church community.

deliver food, what do you do? You pray and act, and who else in your community can better pray and act? Please begin today. Thank you for your prayerful consideration of this challenge.

Sincerely,

Julian Gregori

June, 1997 (updated January, 1998)

Duties of Pastors - A Guide to Dealing With Y2K

1. Evaluate the Y2K evidence,
and discuss the impact it will have on the church

There is no technical evidence in any of the developed nations that utilities, governments or banks will be ready to function at current levels. Current evidence in the US points to the high likelihood of near-complete failure of these three critical services, producing six grave problems:

1. Electrical Power and Phones may be off in most areas for 11 months.

2. Widespread Bank closings may freeze up the worldwide economy for 13 months.

3. Unemployment in urban areas could hit 80% by April, 2000 and last for more than two years.

4. Transportation problems could keep 90% of planes on the ground, 70% of trains frozen to the tracks, and food out of grocery stores for over 10 months. One-fourth of late model cars are predicted to die.

5. Farmers may have a hard time planting and harvesting crops in the 2000-2003 seasons.

6. Crime and disease could be rampant as local services and local government struggle to function without money or dependable utilities, most notably water.

In short, this means your people could be without food, water and the means to obtain it for a period of years. One analyst predicts the hardships will peak in 2004, and last through 2007. Discuss how your

232

household of faith can be cared for, and how your church can be of service to the wider community in an unprecedented opportunity for ministry.

2. Examine the time deadlines for preparation

Storable food and generators will be scarce by January, 1999, and possibly unavailable after March, 1999. Financial disruptions could begin in April, 1999. 1999 crops of non-hybrid seeds should be planted in April and May. Urban real estate prices should begin falling by June, 1999.

3. Immediately decide whether your church will play a role in community leadership and congregational leadership, or not.

Don't defraud the church with indecision, organizational paralysis, or lack of vision. If you decide not to involve the church leaders or congregation in organized preparation, then announce a policy of "every man for himself," providing guidelines to the flock on family responsibility and adequate preparation.

4. Announce your decision to the church immediately, and act accordingly.

If you choose to prepare, your strategy will depend on whether you are in an urban or rural setting, or whether or not you own property in your community. Responsible priorities would include

Assessing the gifts, abilities and assets of each church member

Acquiring stores of food and generator fuel, and appointing stewards of this property

Planning or digging several sources of clean water, pumped by generator

233

Organizing civil defense brigades to assist unprepared people and refugees

Planning future plantings of crops on all available land

Acquiring extra land if needed

Dividing labor and responsibilities between unemployed men

Organizing stores of medical supplies and the help of medical professionals

Converting Church bank assets to gold before April, 1999. Organizing communication channels between leaders, preferably solar HAM radio

Interfacing with local government, including police and National Guard leaders

APPENDIX K

Internet Documentation Resources

Peter DeJager
http://www.year2000.com

Gary North
http://www.remnant.org

Ed Yourdon
http://www.yourdon.com

Westergaard Year 2000
http://www.y2ktimebomb.com

Edward Yardeni
http://www.webcom.com/~yardeni/y2kbook.html

Rick Cowles
http://www.euy2k.com

Government
http://www.comlinnks.com/mmenu.htm

Cassandra Project
http://millennia-bcs.com/cassie.htm

MORE BOOKS

Mother Earth News Bookshelf 800-888-9098

Nitro-Pak Preparedness Center 800-866-4876

Pinetree Garden Seeds 207- 926-3400

Ready Made Resources 800-627-3809

Rodale Press 800-914-9363

HOUSEHOLD ITEMS for Non-Electric Living

Cumberland General Store 800-334-4640

Lehman's Non-Electric 330-857-5757

SURVIVAL SUPPLIES

Nitro-Pak Preparedness Center 800-866-4876

Ready-Made Resources 800-627-3809

Hive Management by Richard Bonney

COOKING

Cooking with the Sun by Beth and Dan Halacy

Marlene's Magic with Food Storage by Marlene Peterson

Just Add Water by Barbara G. Salsbury

Country Beans by Rita Bingham

The TVP Cookbook by Dorothy Bates

Herbal Breads by Ruth Bass

The Bread Book by Ellen Foscue Johnson

Woodstove Cookery by Jane Cooper

FOOD STORAGE

Putting Food By by Greene, Hertzberg and Vaughan

Stocking Up III by Carol Hupping

Keeping the Harvest by Nancy Chioffi

Canning, Freezing, Curing and Smoking by W.F. Eastman

The Busy Person's Guide to Preserving Food by Janet B. Chadwick

Just Add Water by Barbara Salisbury

LIVING OFF THE LAND

Encyclopedia of Country Living by Carla Emery

(NOTE: THIS BOOK IS VERY HIGHLY RECOMMENDED. IF YOU COULD HAVE ONLY ONE BOOK TO HELP YOU LIVE THROUGH Y2K THIS SHOULD BE THE ONE.)

A Bite of Independence by Marilyn Phipps

Creating Covenent Communities by Robert K. Spear

Five Acres and Independence by M. G. Kains

Making the best of the Basics by James Talmage Stevens

Mother Earth News Magazine

Backwoods Home Magazine

Primitive Wilderness Living and Survival Skills

by John and Geri McPherson

The Modern Homestead Manual by Skip Thomsen

Live off the Land in the City and Country by Ragnar Benson

Living without Electricity by Scott and Pellman

HERBAL REMEDIES

From the Shepherd's Purse by Max G. Barlow

The Complete Medicinal Herbal by Penelope Ody

Rodale's Illustrated Encyclopedia of Herbs by Kowalchik and Hylton

Herbs, the Magic Healers by Paul Twitchell

Reader's Digest Magic and Medicine of Plants

MISCELLANEOUS
Into the Primitive -Trapping Techniques by Dale Martin
Knots and How to Tie them by Walter B. Gibson
Basic Butchering of Livestock and Game by John J. Mettler, Jr.
Tan Your Hide by Phyllis Hobson
The Toilet Papers by Sym Van Der Ryn
The Trapper's Bible by Dale Martin
Soap Receipes by Elaine C. White
Humanure Handbook by J. C. Jenkins

NUTRITION
The Nutritional Density of Foods by John Wadsworth
Diet for a Small Planet by Frances Moore Lappe
Receipes for a Small Planet by Ellen Buchman Ewald

SURVIVAL
A Sense of Survival by J. Allen South
Bad Times, Good News by Bill Yatchman
Everybody's Outdoor Survival Guide by Don Paul Teaches
Fighting Chance Ten Feet to Survival by Robinson
How to Bury Your Goods by Eddie the Wire
How to Hide Anything by Michael Connor
Methods of Long-term Underground Storage by Nelson
Poor Man's James Bond by Kurt Saxon
The Big Book of Secret Hiding Places by Jack Lugar
The Survival Retreat by Ragnar Benson
The SAS Survival Handbook by John Wiseman

The Urban Survival Handbook by John Wiseman

The SAS Escape, Evasion and Survival Manual by B.Davies

Wilderness Wayfinding by Bob Newman

Survival Manual by Chris and Gretchen Janowsky

Street-Smart Survival by Victor Santoro

U.S. Army Special Forces Caching Techniques